The Scofield Gang

Melvin Long

The Scofield Gang
Copyright © 2024 by Melvin Long
Front cover illustration by Ellyana Long

Library of Congress Control Number: 2024903061
ISBN-13: Paperback: 978-1-64749-967-9
         ePub: 978-1-64749-968-6

All rights reserved. No part of this publication may be reproduced, distributed, or transmitted in any form or by any means, including photocopying, recording, or other electronic or mechanical methods, without the prior written permission of the publisher or author, except in the case of brief quotations embodied in critical reviews and certain other noncommercial uses permitted by copyright law.

Although every precaution has been taken to verify the accuracy of the information contained herein, the author and publisher assume no responsibility for any errors or omissions. No liability is assumed for damages that may result from the use of information contained within.

Printed in the United States of America

GoToPublish LLC
1-888-337-1724
www.gotopublish.com
info@gotopublish.com

Contents

Chapter I	The Two Communities	1
Chapter II	The Kidnapping	9
Chapter III	The Gang's Halloween Pranks	17
Chapter IV	Christmas Time for Scofield School Children	23
Chapter V	The Threat	27
Chapter VI	The Quarantine	31
Chapter VII	A Foiled Plan	35
Chapter VIII	The Hunt for Chittum Bark	39
Chapter IX	The Purse In The Road Trick	43
Chapter X	The Vine Maple Forest	47
Chapter XI	More Mean Pranks At Tophill By The Gang	51
Chapter XII	The Softball Game	55
Chapter XIII	Summer Vacation	61
Chapter XIV	The County Sheriff Calls At Our House	65
Chapter XV	The Unauthorized Use Of My Uncle's Car	67
Chapter XVI	The Three Ruffians Strike At Tophill Again	73
Chapter XVII	The Gang Of Three Continue Their Pranks At The School	77
Chapter XVIII	Fun On The Ice Ruined By The Ruffians	81
Chapter XIX	We Get a Visit by A Mountain Lion	83
Chapter XX	Grandpa Long Opens a Gas Station	87
Chapter XXI	Strawberry Picking Time	91
Chapter XXII	Back to School	93
Chapter XXIII	The Ruffians Strike at Scofield	97
Chapter XXIV	The Gang Continue Their Pranks at Tophill	101
Chapter XXV	A Wonderful Christmas for Little Mary	103
Chapter XXVI	The Gang Finally Become Good Citizens	105

FOREWORD

While most of the pranks being done by the three young men known as "The Scofield Gang" are the imagination of the author, some actually did happen, such as wiring the doors to the school house closed so no one could get out of the building. The characters in the book are real people that lived in the communities of Scofield and Tophill. These two communities still exist to this day. However, unfortunately, the original school building was torn down several years ago, and it is difficult to determine exactly where the school, the large play shed, the wood shed, and the two outhouses were located on the property. The road leading from Tophill to Scofield is still gravel.

CHAPTER I

The Two Communities

This story occurs in two small communities in Western Oregon, namely Scofield and Tophill. The Gang started terrorizing the Scofield Community and the little one-room school in 1944. In fact, all of the terrorizing events in this story took place during the years 1944 through 1950. Scofield had a small country school comprising grades one through eight. I was in the first grade that year. I'll tell you my name later on in the book. The teacher was a kind woman by the name of Erie E. Ditto. Miss Ditto had never been married, but she did have an adopted daughter and two grandchildren. There were about 27 or 28 students in the school in any given year. At least 50 percent of the students were related and came from the neighboring community, Tophill, which was about three miles from Scofield.

To begin my story, I need to describe the school and the property. There was no electricity in the school, nor were there any inside toilets. The room was lighted by hanging kerosene lamps and large windows on one side of the building. The girl's outhouse was on one side of the property, and the boy's outhouse was on the other side. There was a board fence on the roadside of the property. Next to the school building, there was a large covered play shed with a wooden floor, but no boarded-up sides. Between the play shed and the girl's outhouse stood the May Pole. The playing field was between the girl's outhouse and the road. There was a small play area on the west side of the school building. Directly behind the building, the entire area was covered with blackberry vines. Oh, I almost forgot to mention, there was a small woodshed near the play shed. The road in front of the school was gravel and still is to this day, as I am writing this book. You will see the importance of me giving you all of these details as the story progresses.

Now to begin my story. The Scofield Gang consisted of three young men who had dropped out of school or had been expelled permanently. I doubt they ever spent a day in high school. Their names were Bill, Harley, and Louie. I have no intention of giving their last names, and that's not important anyway. There are lots of Bill's, Harley's and Louie's in the world.

World War II was in its fourth year. I think the three members of the Scofield Gang might have been a little too young for the draft, too bad. Second thought, had they been drafted into the service, none of this probably would have ever happened, and I would not be writing this book.

Before we get too deep into my story, I need to tell you a little bit about these two communities, Scofield and Tophill, since the story takes place in both communities.

Most of the people at Tophill were members of the Long family. Grandpa and Grandma Long had 13 children. Those that were married had families, and they all lived on the hill. The boys married girls from several different families, one of which was a girl named Margaret, my mom. Margaret talked her parents into moving to Tophill, thus they became the only other grandparents on the hill, other than Grandpa and Grandma Long. All the Long family's children attended Scofield School during their grade school years. In fact, 13 or 14 of the Tophill bunch were enrolled at Scofield School in 1944. This is the first year, to my knowledge, the Scofield Gang decided to terrorize the school and both communities.

All the Long family mothers were stay-at-home moms, and the dads worked in the logging and sawmill business, or for the railroad. In fact, the Long brothers built their own sawmill and operated it very successfully for many years, providing a meager living for their families. The children all worked in the strawberry fields in the summer to help their parents by providing additional income for the family. Most of the time, living on the hill, we were like one big happy family. The children would all gather after supper and play different ball games until it was almost too dark to see. Life was pretty carefree and wonderful for all the children. We did not have to worry about iPads, iPhones, Tablets, iPods, homework, video games, drugs, etc. We could roam the hills and forests without worrying about being harmed. We climbed the beautiful fir trees, built forts, and swung from vine and maple trees from tree to tree. In the wintertime, we built igloos when there was enough snow, which, by the way, was nearly every winter. We also played many games in the snow, like Fox and Geese and Snow Tag. Life was never dull for these hillbilly children. We all attended church in a little LDS meeting house in Vernonia, Oregon on Sunday. In fact, the oldest of Grandpa and Grandma Long's thirteen children, my dad, was the spiritual leader of the small congregation. During this time period, neither community had electricity, and the homes or shacks had no inside plumbing. Every home gets its water from a well or spring. Each family had at least one outhouse. The homes were heated with wood and each had a big wood cook stove. Oil or kerosene was used in the lamps or lanterns for lighting. Oh yes, those were the good old days, no utility bills to pay, except for the cost of a gallon or two or kerosene for the lamps.

Another favorite summer pastime for a few of the boys, and some of the girls, was to place objects, like their mother's purse, or a small suitcase, in the middle of the highway with a string attached. When a car would come to a screeching halt, and the driver would attempt to retrieve his prize, the delinquent children would pull the object in quickly and run for their lives through the woods. No driver ever attempted to catch them, as they quickly realized they had been tricked. On one particular evening, I was among the delinquent boys that decided it was a perfect time to pull this mean little trick. The first car that stopped happened to be driven by one of the Scofield Gang, Louie. Unfortunately, I was a little slow at running from behind the stump and Louie got a good look at me. This played an important role in one of the acts of terror that occurred in the school year of 1944-45.

Now a little bit about the Scofield Community. There were no large families like the Longs, but many families, ranging in size from two to four, lived in the community. Louie, Bill, and Harley were in three of these families. Some of the men worked on the railroad that ran through the middle of the community. Some worked in the timber industry, others worked for the highway department. Some were retired grandparents who wanted to be near their grandchildren.

There was a semi-retired dentist, who with his wife and twin girls, moved from Hillsboro to Scofield. It was very handy for many of the local families to have a dentist living in the community. Not only did the residents of Scofield take advantage of him being in the community, but also the Tophill folks. On more than one occasion kids from The Hill would walk all the way to Dr. Brown's place to have dental work done, a distance of about three miles. Usually that meant getting an aching tooth pulled. If Dr. Brown was working in the field or in the barn he would come in, take off his gumboots, wash his hands thoroughly and proceed with what needed to be done to his young patient, and then the child or children would walk home. The Novocaine would usually last until the children got about half way home. I was one of those patients on more than one occasion.

Most of the Scofield children had to walk to school, but the Tophill kids all rode the school bus, as did the teacher, Miss Ditto.

There were no churches in either community so the local church goers would go to Church in either Vernonia or Buxton. The only thing that ever brought the two communities together was the school. There was no Grange, Community Hall or Fire Station in either community. There were no paved roads in the entire community of Scofield. The freight and passenger trains that passed through both communities was the highlight of many days, especially if it brought an unexpected guest to the area. Once the children from each community arrived at school, they were like one big family. The kids wore one another's coats or sweaters, and shared one another's combs, if they had one. The children all brought cold lunches to school, and these were shared on many occasions. Generally speaking, the Scofield kids had better lunches, at least it seemed that way to the Tophill children.

If one child came to school with head lice the entire school ended up with head lice. All the childhood diseases were spread throughout both communities, such as Chicken-Pox, Measles, Mumps, Common Flu, etc. There were no vaccines for these diseases in those days. Most folks in both communities were on about the same economic level, poor and dirt poor, but we all were rich in so many other ways. We never thought of ourselves as being poor.

The Scofield Community had an active 4-H Club and many of the school children from both communities participated from time to time. There was also an active Boy Scout Troop, with a Mr. George Berge as the Scout Master. Boys from both communities made up the troop.

The Second World War was going on, so many evenings we would have to put newspaper over our windows, in the event enemy planes would fly over. It was hoped they would not be able to see our community.

Now to continue with the story of the Scofield Gang: school started as usual the day after Labor Day of 1944.

As she did every year, Miss Ditto always spent the first hour of the first day teaching the children how to evacuate the building in case of a fire. There were about 27 or 28 children enrolled in grades one through eight. The older, and in most cases the taller children, were lined up at the back of the group, with the first graders being in the very front row. Miss Ditto always demanded all the students to be absolutely quiet, so that everyone could receive her detailed instruction as to what to do in case of a fire. One of the older boys decided that he was not going to be that quiet, as he had something he wanted to whisper to his friend who was standing next to him. Miss Ditto gave him a very stern look and sharp reprimand. Me, the little boy from Tophill mentioned earlier in the book, the one involved in the purse trick, was in the front row. This was my very first day in the first grade. Being a very spoiled child and a mama's boy, I really did not want to go to school on that very first day. I was very timid, shy, and very scared. I thought Miss Ditto was scolding me so I decided to end my school career right then and there.

I ran out the front door, grabbed my lunch pail, coat, and hat in the foyer, and headed for home, a distance of about three miles. It just so happened that Louie, one of the three members of the Scofield Gang, who lived close to the school, was going out to the mail box. He recognized me right away. This was a perfect opportunity to teach this little delinquent a lesson. Louie grabbed me, and placed his hand over my mouth so that no one could hear my screaming. He immediately blindfolded me and took me into the forest behind Harley and Bill's house, where the other two gang members joined him. This is where the first act of terror in the story begins.

Miss Ditto And A Few Of Her Students

Chapter II

The Kidnapping

Louie said, "Bill and Harley, do you remember me telling you about the little delinquent brat from Tophill that pulled the purse trick on me on highway 47 early this summer?" Harley said, "Sure but what does that have to do with this little scoundrel?" Louie said, "This is the very boy that I saw running from behind the stump." Harley said, "Are you sure about that?" "Oh yes," Louie replied. "I could never forget the face of that little rat." By this time Louie had removed his hand from over my mouth, but I was too terrified to scream, as I supposed that no one could hear me anyway. I was trembling and sobbing almost uncontrollably. I just knew that mom and dad would never see me alive again.

Louie suggested they tie me up to a small vine maple tree while they held a 'gang meeting' some distance away, in which they would discuss what to do with me to teach me a lesson. At last, I could breathe a small sigh of relief in hearing this. They were going to teach me a lesson, but at least they were not going to kill me, I hoped. With this, I stopped crying and just tried to take deep breaths. After a while, in what seemed to be hours, but probably not more than 45 minutes, they came back with three small sacks full of things like donuts, bananas, peanut butter sandwiches, cans of Pepsi, etc. They all had big hunting knives attached to their belts. I also noticed that Louie was wearing a gun belt with a pistol in the holster. They sat down on the ground all around me and gorged on the food. By this time, it was nearly noon and I was really starting to get hungry, but I would not have taken any food from them, even had they offered some. I just wanted them to get through with their torture of me, and take me back to the road, so I could go back to school, before it was time to catch the school bus to go home, and into the arms of my dear parents. And then a terrifying thought came to me. What if they just leave me tied to this tree? I consoled myself by thinking, surely, they can't be that mean. Even if they did, I knew I could work loose as they had not tied me very tightly. If I got loose, I had no idea of how we got here, as they had tied a towel around my head and over my eyes.

After they finished eating, and having some discussion, they left again. I heard them talking amongst themselves about what they might do with me for the rest of the day. Their conversation went something like this:

Louie said, "Bill and Harley, what do think we should do with this little twerp to teach him not to mess with any of us ever again?" Harley said, "I think we should leave him out here 'til just before dark, and then take him out to the road and release him. By that time, there will be people looking for him. We will have to be very careful not be seen with this little juvenile cry baby." Bill said, "We will threaten him by telling him that bad things will happen to his family if he tells anyone our names." Louie agreed with the plan.

By this time, I was sure that school was out for the day. The thought came to me that Miss Ditto probably thought that I had walked all the way home. Not having any phones in either community, there was no way that she could get word to my parents unless a parent or member of the community stopped by the school. I knew that when I did not get off the school bus my mother would be alarmed and terrified. She would go to my Aunt Alice's house immediately. Since my Aunt Alice had a car and could drive, I was sure they would start searching for me right away. They couldn't do very much until my father got home from the sawmill at 5:00 p.m., as mom had small children to care for. She could take them over to my Grandmother Bailey's house if she was at home.

All of these thoughts were running through my little mind. Thank goodness they occupied a lot of my time. All of the time I was praying and asking God to help me get home safe. I was so thankful that my parents had taught me to pray since I was two or three years old. I started thinking about my new little baby brother, Delbert, who was only about 5 months old. I wandered if I would ever see him or my sisters again? I thought about my dear Grandma Bailey. Would I ever be able to set on her lap again, and have her tell me stories about growing up in South Africa and Holland. A lot of things run through one's mind when he is not sure what is going to happen to him in the next few hours or days.

The gang members never came back until the sun had gone down. I was starting to get a little cold, and I was not able to put my coat on. They brought more food with them, and seemed to enjoy surrounding me and gorging themselves with all their goodies. Louie asked me if I was hungry. I said, "Yes, but I don't want any of your rotten food. I just want to go home, so would you please untie me and take me out to the road. I am sure my parents are looking for me." Harley said, "If you shut up, we probably will cut you lose from the tree when it gets dark." Bill said, "You little brat, we are warning you that if you ever mention our names to anyone, bad things will happen to your family. We know where you live, you are part of those weird Mormons that live at Tophill. In fact, you are the one that ran from behind the stump when Louie stopped to pick up that woman's purse from the middle of the road early in the summer." By this time, I was starting to relax a little more and not be so frightened, since they told me they were going to release me. I started to laugh a little and said, "That was a pretty good trick, wasn't it?" Boy, was that a mistake on my part. Bill came up behind me and kicked me in my rear end as hard as he could. By that time, I had determined that I was not going to cry again. They seemed to enjoy seeing me cry.

Harley retrieved his huge hunting knife from the scabbard and flashed it in front of me. With a hateful grin on his face he asked, "How would you like to have a slash across your right ear?" That really scared me, but I tried not to let it show. Bill came over and kicked me again in the seat of my pants. Louie said, "Come on boys, it's time we let him go." Harley suggested they point me in the direction of the road and then scatter. Bill told me to walk in a straight line, and I should reach the road in about 1/2 hour. With that, Louie came over and untied me. Boy was I happy to have my hands free and to be untied from the tree. The first thing I did was to put on my coat and hat.

I said a quick silent prayer and headed out. There was still a little daylight left. Fortunately, I stumbled onto an old logging road right away. I remembered seeing an old road bed just before the rail road crossing about 1/2 mile from the school. I hoped this was that road. I couldn't run, as there were too many limbs and small trees that had fallen across the old road bed. After about one-half hour I did reach the county road. Boy, was I relieved! I started running in the direction I thought would lead me to the school. I had only walked about five minutes when I saw a car approaching. I stepped to the side of the road and waited patiently. As it got closer, I could see that it was a police car. When it pulled up by my side, my father was the first one out of the car. I cried with joy and he had tears also.

"Son, you are safe and our prayers have been answered." He held me for several minutes. The officer just let us stand there for several minutes. I heard him go on his police radio and tell the officer at the command center that they had found me, and that I appeared to be ok. My dad said, "We will discuss what happened when we got back to the school where the command center has been set up." It took us several minutes to get back to the school. The logging road that I had followed was not the one I thought it was. It came out about one mile past the Berge house, which was only about one mile from U.S. Highway 26, near the tunnel.

When we got to the school my mother and my Aunt Alice and several men were still out searching for me. Everyone had previously agreed to meet back at the command center at 9:00 p.m. It was now 8:45 p.m. Mom and Aunt Alice pulled up in front of the school. Mom was crying and held me for several minutes. She said, "Your brothers and sisters are at Grandma's house. We did not tell them where we were going. They were all crying when we left, but Grandma Bailey told them that things would turn out ok." The sheriff in charge said, "You folks can go on home now, I will come to your house in the morning around 9:00 a.m. to get details of what happened." I just wanted to get home as I was very, very tired and hungry. Dad asked the relatives not to come over to the house in the morning, not until after we had talked to the Sheriff.

When we got to Grandma's house, she had supper waiting for us. I was so tired that I nearly fell asleep while I was eating. Grandma had homemade bread and my very favorite, raisin pie.

Prior to going to bed we all knelt down by my parent's bed and my dad offered a prayer of thanks for my safe return. Dad said, "We will discuss the details of the event in the morning when the Sheriff comes. Right now, your little brother needs to get some rest. He is very tired and has had a very traumatic day."

I did not wake up the next morning until almost 8:00 a.m. Mom had my favorite breakfast prepared, French toast. Dad stayed home from work, so he could be there when the Sheriff arrived. Deputy Barnes arrived about 9:00 a.m. We all sat around the kitchen table. The deputy asked if he could just have dad, mom and me in the room for the interview. My brothers and sisters went over to Grandma Bailey's house. Deputy Barnes asked, "Will it be ok if I record the interview?" Dad said, "Sure."

Deputy Barnes asked me to tell in my own words what happened from the time I left the school until I was picked up last night. I went into as much detail as I could but I did not reveal the names of the three men, as I feared for the safety of my family. My brothers and sisters did not go to school that day. I was still pretty upset and I cried often, as I was talking with the deputy. I hoped that I would be able to go back to school on Monday. Right now, I just wanted to be with my parents, and to be home with my brothers and sisters. I was glad this was Friday. We got a pleasant surprise in the evening. Miss Ditto had driven her car to school today, just so she could come by our house to see how I was doing. Normally she rode the same school bus the children did. Her home was in Banks, Oregon, near the high school. Dad thanked her for coming by, and told her that his school age children would be back in school on Monday. She gave me a big hug before she left. Needless to say, that made me very happy. She also said, "Melvin, I want you to know that I was not scolding you, but your cousin Duane." That made me feel even better. I then had to tell my parents why I had left school. I also assured them that I had learned my lesson, and that that would never happen again.

Dad and Mom never did discuss with me anything related to the investigation of this traumatic event. They never pressured me into revealing the names of the men that held me captive. I think they had a good idea who they were, as these men were well known throughout both communities and surrounding areas.

We had a good weekend at home, and I was able to spend time playing with my cousins. Of course, they all wanted to know what had happened to me when I left school on Thursday morning. I gave them brief accountings. I really did not want to go into a lot of detail. We all went to church in Vernonia on Sunday. My father gave a brief statement of what had happened, but he asked that members not approach me with questions or comments. I was relieved, as I really did not want to discuss the event with anyone. I hoped to be able to put this out of my mind as soon as possible, and just get back to my normal, peaceful life.

I, along with my brothers and sisters, returned to school on Monday. Believe it or not, Miss Ditto continued with the fire drill, because she wanted me to know what to do in case of a fire in the old wood frame building.

We had a long and beautiful fall in Western Oregon. I started to enjoy school. I was so happy to be learning to read. Miss Ditto spent most of her time teaching the first, second, and third graders the three R's.

CHAPTER III

The Gang's Halloween Pranks

Halloween is always a special time for folks living in both Scofield and Tophill. The small children do the traditional things, while many of the adult men are more interested in pulling tricks on their neighbors, particularly the elderly.

The Scofield Gang decided they would celebrate Halloween a day early, and their target was to be the community where their first victim lived. They didn't know the house that I lived in so, they decided to hit as many places as they could.

Harley said, "Louie, show Bill and me the place on Highway 47 where that little juvenile brat pulled the purse trick on you." The Gang decided that they would start with the house nearest to that spot. After driving by a couple of times Louie spotted the stump, so he was able to identify the spot. He got mad all over again and said, "I'll get revenge on his family by tipping their outhouse over tonight." Harley and Bill said, "We're not going to stop with one outhouse, let's tip over every outhouse in the community. We just have to be very careful and not get caught." Louie said, "Where should we hide our car?" They decided to hide their car just past the last house in the community, which was on Nowakowski Road.

They started their little acts of terror just a little after midnight. There was a full moon, so they had no trouble seeing. The gang moved quietly and quickly until they got to the last house. Just as they were approaching the outhouse, the back door of the main house opened and a man with a shotgun came out. The men froze in their tracks. Fortunately, for them the outhouse was between them and the man. They remained very still for several minutes until they were sure the man had gone back inside. As they were about to begin their dirty work, Louie decided he would take a quick look inside the privy. When he grabbed hold of the metal door handle, he let out a scream. The handle was evidently hooked up to a hot electric wire. With that the back door to the main house swung open and out came a huge German Shepherd dog. The gang members ran for their lives. Fortunately, for them their car was close by, as the outhouse was right next to the gravel road. As Louie was about to get into the car, the dog caught hold of his leg and took a chunk of flesh. He managed to get into the back seat of the car, and Harley, the driver, sped away with the dog following the car for several hundred feet. As it turned out, the only other outhouse in the community that did not get tipped over was the one belonging to their first victim's parents. My dad was tired of our outhouse getting tipped over every year, so he purchased a new car battery and wired it to the metal handle on the door, just like his brother Oscar had done. Oh, how I wish they would have come to our house. Evidently, they could not find our outhouse, as it sat right behind our wood shed.

When the gang got way down the road, Harley stopped the car, as Louie's leg was bleeding quite badly. Bill took off his shirt and placed it over the wound to stop the bleeding. All the time Louie was screaming with pain. After they got to Bill's house Louie had finally stopped screaming and the bleeding had stopped. Louie said, "I can hardly wait for this leg to heal; I will definitely get my revenge on that devil of a dog. He will be a dead dog!"

Needless to say, there were a lot of mad dads the next morning. There was a lot of accusing going on. Grandpa Long had 10 sons and they all lived in the community. Grandpa

Long decided he would take charge of the questioning. He invited each son to come to his and grandma's house. Each one gave the same answer. "Dad we had nothing to do with this dastardly act." There were a few other men in the community, but they were not suspect. Grandpa Bailey was 70 years old. Alf Carlson was not the type to pull such a mean trick. Ed Everett was too kind to ever cause any one extra work at home. The truth be known, most of the younger unmarried Long boys were disappointed, in that they would not be able to perform their usual Halloween tricks, like harnessing Grandpa Bailey's cow and hooking it up to his hay wagon, soaping car windows, tipping over outhouses, etc.

In a few days life in the community got back to normal, the children had a great Halloween night of trick-or-treat, and the outhouse ordeal was soon forgotten. No one in the community ever suspected that the 'night before Halloween' visitor was not even a member of their community. The Scofield Gang got away with another act of terror, but not without a serious dog bite to Louie's leg.

The next act of terror involved the rail road which ran through the middle of the Scofield community. There was a long spur which was necessary for trains to be able to pass one another on the long trip to Tillamook. Of course, this involved having a switch, which in those days was operated manually, to divert one train onto the spur so the other train going in the opposite direction could pass. It's a good thing the trains were always going fairly slow during this part of their journey, as there were hills and sharp curves, in light of what was about to happen on November 1, of 1944.

The Gang was having lunch together at Harley's house, when Bill said, "Hey Harley and Louie, you know we have been pretty quiet lately and it's getting pretty boring around here. I've been thinking a lot lately about pulling a little trick on that cranky old train engineer that comes through on

Monday morning on his way to Tillamook. Last Monday he yelled at me, and he used some pretty foul words when he told me to walk faster when I crossed the tracks, as the train was approaching the crossing. Luckily, he could not hear what I said back to him." Harley said, "Bill, what do you have in mind?" Bill said, "What do you think about moving the switch that diverts the train onto the spur when another train needs to pass? The engineer won't be expecting anything unusual." "Wow! Will he ever get an unpleasant surprise?" Louie said, "Bill, you are so smart, I think that is exactly what we should do. Are you in, Harley?" Harley said, "I can hardly wait. When should we do this?" The gang decided they would move the switch late Sunday night, well after dark.

On Sunday night the gang met near the rail road track switch. Harley said, "Bill, since your dad used to work for the railroad, why don't you operate the switch? Louie and I will stand guard and warn you if a car approaches." "Sounds good to me," replied Bill. Prior to returning to their respective homes the gang decide on a location to meet Monday morning so they could watch their act of terror unfold. All three told their parents they had a day job in Forest Grove on Monday.

Bill drove to Harley and Louie's house and picked them up. They drove down to Buxton to have breakfast at Staley's restaurant. The waitress greeted them as they entered the restaurant and said,

"Where are you guys going so early in the morning?" Louie said, "We have a day job in Forest Grove pouring cement, so we needed to have a good breakfast." Nothing more was said, and after the gang finished their breakfast, they left the restaurant. No one noticed the direction they took as they turned west onto US Hwy 26.

They headed west for about seven miles, turned right on Scofield Road, and drove towards their designated hiding spot. Louie looked at his watch and observed that it was 7:30 a.m. In the meantime, Engineer Rod Stevens boarded the S.P. & S. Engine in Portland at 5:00 a.m. and headed west towards Tillamook. He made good time as the train had no load. They were to pick up lumber from a large mill near Tillamook and return the next day.

George Berge got up early and decided he would run his little speeder car from Scofield, for about 10 miles, toward Tillamook, as there had been some pretty strong winds during the night. He wanted to make sure the track was clear, as he knew the Monday morning freight train was due around 8:00 a.m. George looked at his watch, it was 7:00 a.m. He moved his speeder car onto the tracks about one half mile east of the switch. As he approached the switch, he noticed that it did not look to be in the right position. As he was traveling very slowly, he was able to stop without any trouble. He quickly put the switch where it belonged and continued on his journey. He never even gave it a thought that perhaps someone had intentionally moved the switch. He could hear the whistle of the train at each crossing. He knew that it was at least a couple of miles away. It was moving slowly up the steep grade from Buxton.

The Scofield Gang arrived at their hiding place at 7:45 a.m. They waited anxiously for the train to arrive at the switch. As Engineer Rod approached the Scofield Road crossing, he blew the whistle three times. The gang could hardly control their excitement. Their hiding place was only a short distance from the switch. They were hiding behind a huge old growth stump. The minutes ticked by as their excitement quickened. Bill said, "What do we do if the train is not able to stop by the time it reaches the end of the spur? Our hiding place, this old stump, is only a short distance from the end of the spur." Louie said, "We run down the hill, away from the tracks, as fast as we can." Harley piped up and said, "It could be pretty bad if the engine plows into this old stump, crew members could be seriously hurt."

Engineer Rod pushed the throttle as far forward as it would go, as this stretch of the track was a good place to make up a little lost time from climbing the long uphill grade from Buxton. There were several school children waiting in front of their homes as the train sped by. Rod and the train conductor always brought candy bars along on their Monday morning trip. I had spent the night with my friend Bobby Berge, so I was excited to get this special treat in my lunch on Monday morning. They never returned to Portland with any of the candy. Before long the train was out of sight, and the children all had candy to take to school and share with their friends.

The gang members were absolutely horrified. Louie and Harley immediately swore and yelled at Bill. Bill assured them that he had moved the switch correctly. Harley said, "Bill, you will pay for this failure. You probably should not be part of our gang for a very long while." Louie said, "Oh Harley, why don't you cool it? I am sure we will have another chance to get even with that grumpy old engineer." Little did they know this was the final run on this particular route for Engineer Rod Stevens. He was being transferred to the Portland/Spokane - Washington run.

CHAPTER IV

Christmas Time for Scofield School Children

Scofield School Students 1945

December was the month all the children at Scofield School loved the best. Every year, Miss Ditto prepared the children for a Christmas program. They did school work in the morning, and the afternoon was spent practicing for the program. The program always had a Nativity scene with the children as live actors. The choir consisted of all the students. Several beautiful Christmas songs were sung by the children, with parents and other guests joining in on the last verse of Silent Night. There was always a jolly old Santa Claus that brought caramel popcorn balls, oranges, gum and a new pencil for each child in attendance. The parents from both communities always attended the Christmas program, as did most of the other members of the communities.

Being in first grade I was always in the front row. Right away I spotted the Scofield Gang members in the audience. They were with their parents. Bill spotted me first and alerted his criminal friends, Louie and Harley. I think they decided to attempt to ruin my evening. All three stared at me throughout the entire program. I decided that I would pay no attention to them. I just kept looking out towards the audience and smiling. I could tell they were really irritated that I didn't show any fear or concern that they were there. When the program was over, we were instructed by Miss Ditto to return to our seats in the back of the room. Louie happened to be sitting at the end of the isle, and as I walked by, he stuck his foot out very slyly and tripped me. I fell to the floor but got up quickly. Very few people saw me fall, and I acted as though nothing had happened. I stayed close to my parents the rest of the evening. Fortunately, the gang left as soon as the program ended.

Snow started falling on the first day of our Christmas vacation, which was December 19th. It snowed every day for the next 5 days, so by Christmas day we had almost three feet of snow. We were all so happy to be out of school and to have a white Christmas. My cousins, brothers and sisters, and I built igloos, played snow games, had snowball fights, and in general had such a great time during the entire vacation. Our Grandma and Grandpa Bailey made sure we children had things under our Christmas tree. Dad never had enough money to buy presents, as it was all he could do to provide the other necessities of life, like food, clothing, shelter, and adequate transportation for the family of six children. Fortunately, the Scofield Gang left us alone during the entire vacation, for which I was very thankful.

December the 26, 1944 was a sad day for all of the Long family. Our dear Uncle Lawrence had joined the Navy recently, and had to leave for Boot Camp in Farragut, Idaho. The war was raging in the Pacific and Europe as well. We all loved Uncle Larry so very much. He always had a car, and would load several of us in his car and take us to a movie in Portland. You could see two or three movies for 25 cents. I will never forget seeing all of my brothers and sisters and cousins crying as he went around and hugged each one. Grandpa and Grandma Long, and all of his brothers and sisters were there to see him off. Uncle Larry assured us that he would be back after the war was over. For the next several years we only heard from our parents' little tidbits of information about our dear uncle. We were so happy and excited when the war finally ended in 1945. Uncle Larry was given an honorable discharge and returned home in January of 1946

School resumed on the second day after New Year's. I was excited to see my friends from Scofield, particularly Bobby Berge. He and I were the only boys in the first grade. My cousin Alice Louise was the only girl. Of course, we all had to show off new clothes that were Christmas presents. I was very proud of the new hat my Grandma Bailey had given me. Bobby had all-new clothes, most of which he informed me his mother had made. Most of the girls wore cute dresses they had received, and some whose parents seemed to have more money, had new beautiful coats.

During the vacation Miss Ditto made little presents for each child in the school. She gave each of us our present at the end of the first day back.

There was still a lot of snow on the ground which made for a lot of fun at recess time. The hill on the north side of the school building provided an excellent place for us slide down. We would take pieces of card board or old gunnysacks to sit on, and away we would go down the hill. We stopped just as we approached the side of the school building. Those children that didn't want to get cold and wet would play in the covered play shed on the south side of the school building. We had a recess in the morning and one in the afternoon. Life was so simple then, especially for the children. Our playground was the entire neighborhood we lived in. It seems as though the only trouble causers in our two communities were the three members of the Scofield Gang.

CHAPTER V

The Threat

Their next little prank involved the school building and it happened several weeks prior to spring vacation. This one was evidently Louie's idea. Louie happened to run into Harley and Bill at Howard Score's store in Buxton Sunday evening. Louie said, "Harley and Bill why don't you come over to my place later this evening? I have a plan I want to present to you about some fun we could have with the school building." "Sure Louie, how about 8:00 p.m. tonight?" "That sounds good, my parents usually go to bed by that time on Sunday night because, they both have to get up early Monday morning."

Harley and Bill arrived at 8:00 p.m. Bill said, "Ok Louie, tell us your plan." Louie spent the next 15 or 20 minutes going over the plan, which was to wire the two doors leading outside the school building closed. He reminded Bill and Harley that none of the windows were made to open. So, no one from inside would be able to leave the building. Bill said he would muffle his voice and tell Miss Ditto that they were going set the building on fire if any one tried to escape by breaking a window. The last item of business was to decide on a date to perform their criminal act of terror. It was decided to do it on the Friday before spring vacation, which was only five days away. During the week Louie collected several strands of barbed wire.

The Scofield Gang arrived at the school about 9:30 a.m. They walked from their homes as they did not want to be seen in their cars near the school. They spent about twenty minutes wiring the doors closed. And then they waited for the first student to try to leave the building to go to the outhouse.

Wouldn't you know it, I was the first one to ask Miss Ditto if I could go to the toilet. When I tried to open the door, it would not open. I was almost too embarrassed to go back and tell the teacher that I could not open the door, but I had to go so bad that I had no other choice but to solicit her help. All the other students started snickering and making fun of me. This didn't help matters at all. I almost started crying, but the teacher shut the inside door leading to the foyer so they could not see what was going on. She tried to open the door but of course was not able to.

In the meantime, Louie, Bill, and Harley were outside, and with muffled voices they were laughing and saying mean things. This really made Miss Ditto angry. We went back inside and the teacher told the rest of the students what was going on. With that, several students came to me and said they were sorry for making fun of me. Miss Ditto told me to go in the back room and use an old chamber pot that was there for special occasions when students might not be able to go to the regular toilet. Needless to say, I was embarrassed. I made sure the door to the back room was closed.

After getting everyone settled down, Miss Ditto told us just to resume our studies and act like nothing was wrong. She assured us that things were going to turn out ok, and that she would break one of the windows if the doors were not unwired by bus time at the end of the day. All of this time the gang members were hiding behind the building and planning their next step of this little act of terror. When they heard a car stop out in front of the school they scattered into the adjoining woods and headed for their homes.

Mrs. Atwood happened to drive by the school a few minutes after 12:00 p.m. and noticed that there were no children outside for their noon recess, so she decided to stop and see what was going on. She had something that she wanted to discuss with Miss Ditto, as she was the local 4-H club leader, and they were planning an event during spring break. When she got to the door, she immediately saw that it was wired shut. She had no gloves with her, and it was very difficult to unwind the wire. In the process she got several pokes from the barbs, and her hands were bleeding in several places. This did not stop her, and in a few minutes, she was inside the building. Miss Ditto and the children were very happy to greet her, particularly her son Wayne.

Miss Ditto sent several of the older boys outside to see if anyone was hiding behind the school building or inside either of the out houses. They came back and reported they had not found anyone. With that the teacher told all of the students they could go outside, and that she would give them an extra-long noon recess. Mrs. Atwood asked Miss Ditto if she wanted to report this to the Sheriff, but her reply was, "No, these are just some neighborhood boys that have nothing better to do. I have a good idea who they are and I am going to take the matter up with their parents in the next few days." "Since there will be no school next week, I will drive my car here and have a visit with their parents."

Of course, the children all had a big story to tell their parents when they got home. My Aunt Alice was on the School Board and she said she was going to look into the matter. That is the last time I heard anything about what took place. I imagine that my aunt talked to Miss Ditto and she probably assured her that she would handle the matter.

We were all very happy to be out of school for a week. We had a late snow storm the first part of the week. Top Hill got about 12 inches of snow. This could not have come at a better time. We built igloos, played snow games, had snowball fights and so much more. Building an igloo was no small task. First, it was necessary to pile the snow and then pack it down into square blocks. We would move these blocks together and stack them as high as we could. Next, we would get boards and place across the top, then pile a lot of snow on top of the boards. We made a hole in the top so that when we placed our small King Heater inside, we would have a hole for the chimney. We would then collect old rags, coats, quilts and gunny sacks to place on the ground. We would then build a small fire in the stove, eat our lunch, and stay in the igloo until it started to melt. With a small fire it might last for a few days. We put the fire out each day, and piled more snow on top.

The week went by all too quickly, but in a way most of the children were happy to see their school friends again. A new family, the Jackson's, moved into the school district, in fact they moved into a vacant house right across from the school. There were several children in the family of school age. They were all real nice kids and easy to make friends with. Before long we were all sharing hats, coats, and lunches with our new found friends, just as we always did with one another before they arrived.

CHAPTER VI

The Quarantine

Within a couple of weeks Aunt Alice discovered head lice in her children's hair. She alerted my parents and they discovered that we all had head lice. With that, the County Health Nurse came out to the school and examined each child's hair. There were only two or three that didn't have the lice. The Heath Nurse ordered the school closed for two weeks, to give our parents time to rid all of us of these little creatures.

Aunt Alice came over to our house to discuss the situation with my parents. The conversation went something like this: "Charles and Margaret, since we have the largest families, and I know you have your hands full Margaret, I would like to volunteer to treat all of the Top Hill girls to rid them of the lice. Each girl will need to come to my house every day, and I will help them with washing their hair with a special shampoo." My mom thought that was a splendid idea. She said, "Thank you so much, my girls have been crying, fearing that they would have to have all of their heads shaved." Aunt Alice said, "You can assure them that will not be necessary, but for the boys, that is the quickest and surest way to rid them of these little nasty creatures. I have noticed that most of the boys already wear very short hair." Mom said, "When would you like me to send our girls over?" "Right away" replied Aunt Alice. "It will probably take several washings to make sure they are all free from the lice." When mom called the girls in and told them the good news, they were so happy. All four of my sisters rushed over to our aunt's house that very evening to start the process. For my sisters this was probably the first time they had ever used shampoo. Shampoo was a luxury item at our house. We normally used plain old bar soap.

Each of my uncles, that had sons, always cut their boy's hair, so this was not an issue. Aunt Alice did talk with each of her brothers and tell them what needed to be done. She managed to get all of the girl's hair shampooed the first time by the next evening. She gave the girls a schedule of when they should come. This process went on for almost two weeks. All of the boys had shaved heads within a couple of days.

Aunt Alice called the County Health Nurse and asked her to contact the family that was responsible for this outbreak. She assured her that had already been done.

This gave The Scofield Gang a great opportunity to do a lot of little mischievous things on the school property. The first thing they did was to remove the merry-go-around from its anchoring post. They painted the Maypole black. They put colored wax on the lower windows of the school building.

Fortunately, the school custodian came to make some minor repairs on the play shed the second week of the closure. He was able to put the merry-go-around back on its anchor post. He also removed the colored wax from the windows, but he decided to leave the maypole black.

School was able to resume on schedule. The County Health Nurse was there to examine each child for head lice. Only one case of lice was found, and that was on the oldest Jackson girl. She had refused to allow her mom to cut her hair short. The nurse was very kind to her, and said that she would talk to her mom, and help with a treatment that would rid her of the lice in a couple of days. She was a very pretty girl, and my cousin, Duane, had a crush on her, so he was happy when the nurse said she would be back in school in a couple of days.

We were all very happy to be back in school, and to be with our friends. It was early spring, and it rained every day we were home so, needless to say, we were all very bored with being confined to our home's day in and day out. At school we had a huge covered play shed, and we got three recesses each day, so we were outside a lot.

Things in the little communities of Scofield and Tophill were pretty quiet during the rest of March and part of April. I do remember one morning being very different from the rest of the days of April. We were all working on our lessons for our morning classes when a knock came to the front door. Miss Ditto opened the door, and there stood Mrs. Fellas, with tears running down her cheeks. She asked Miss Ditto to step into the coat room and shut the door. She then told Miss Ditto that she had just heard on the radio that President Roosevelt had just had a stroke and was in the hospital. When Miss Ditto came back into the room, she told us that the President of the United States was very ill and had to be admitted to the hospital. We were all very sad, particularly the older children.

It rained most every day, so the children were pretty much confined to their homes, the school building, and the play shed. Weekends were always fun, as this was a time for going to church, visiting our relatives in other nearby towns, and staying up late. We children got to listen to our favorite radio programs, such as The Lone Ranger, Sky King, Sergeant Preston of The Yukon, Lassie, and many others. The older girls in our community, those in the seventh and eighth grades, would get into their mother's make-up drawer, apply some make-up, and organize little dance parties in their homes. My aunt Alice had a battery-operated phonograph that played 45 records. She would loan it to her daughter, Willina, who would then provide the music for the dance.

Believe me, there was never one single boy in attendance at these parties. It was very common in those days for girls and women to dance with one another. Never the case with men or boys!

It stopped raining in the last week of April, and we were greeted with warm sunshine for several days in a row. The trees started to bud out, and the sound of frogs could be heard every evening. We all got 'spring fever' and could hardly wait for summer vacation.

Evidently, the warmer weather got the Scofield Gang guys in the mood to start their little acts of terror in the communities again. It seems as though their favorite target now was the school. It was close to their homes, and no one was ever around on weekends. It was on one of these weekends that Louie made a visit to his two cohorts, Bill and Harley, to make plans for their next adventure.

CHAPTER VII

A Foiled Plan

Louis said, "Hey guys what do you thing about having a little fun at the school grounds tonight?" Bill said, "You know I have been thinking the same thing." Harley got very excited and chimed in with, "I have a suggestion Bill and Louie, why don't we board up the entrances to the school's outhouses?" Bill said, "Harley you are so smart, I think that would be so much fun. I hope that little rat that played the purse trick on Louie, is the first one that needs to go." The rest of the day was spent getting boards from their father's old lumber piles, getting nails and hammers together, and lying to their parents about what they were planning. The excuse all three gave was, that they were building a fort in the woods behind the school house, but not on school property. This allowed them to store their materials just off the school property in case someone came by and asked what they were doing. The gang loaded all the materials into Bill's father's pickup, and they made a quick stop on the side road by the school, where they unloaded the materials in a hurry.

At dusk, the trio walked through the school yard to the spot where they had stashed the materials. Louie brought a lantern, but did not light it until it got too dark to see. Harley said, "Bill, you hold the boards in place and I will nail them to the outhouse walls. We must work fast, as my father will be going by on his way home from work, around 10:00 p.m. Louie, all I need you to do is hold the lantern." Things were progressing quite well until Harley let out a deafening scream. He missed a nail head and the full force of the hammer came down on his thumb. His thumb was bleeding, and upon closer examination his entire thumb nail was broken and smashed. He could no longer do the nailing so he traded places with Louie. Harley was not very much help the rest of the evening.

When they got half way through the project with the boy's outhouse, they discovered they only had enough boards to do one outhouse. This made Louie mad, and he lashed out at Bill and Harley. He said "I told you guys that we would need more material to do both outhouses, but you both assured me that we had plenty." Bill came right back with, "Louie, you always want to blame Harley and me when something goes wrong with our plans. You never accept any of the responsibility when things don't go the way you think they should go." With that, Harley chimed in, "Louie perhaps you would like to finish this little project yourself." Louie came back with, "Let's stop arguing and get this project done. We can do the girls outhouse tomorrow night." Both Bill and Harley said, "Ok, but stop getting on our case every time something goes wrong."

The gang finished the boy's outhouse project about 9:45 p.m. and then headed down to Buxton to get some "spirits". When they got back to Louie's place, Louie said, "Can you both be at my house by noon tomorrow, so we can finish tearing down another old building that my dad wants to get rid of? There will be plenty of material to finish our outhouse projects." Both Bill and Harley said, "Yes."

The gang spent most of Sunday afternoon tearing down the old building on Louie's place, and hauling the materials to the place where they could be easily retrieved when it got dark. Another argument caused Bill and Harley to threaten Louie with not helping to finish the project. It seems as though Louie wanted Bill and Harley to drive down to Buxton to get some 'spirits,' while he would make sure no one bothered their stash of materials. Bill and Harley knew the real reason Louie wanted them to go to Buxton, was so that he could go home and sleep the rest of the afternoon. It was finally decided that all three would make the trip to Buxton.

The story gets even better with what happened on their way home from Buxton. As they rounded the corner on Highway 47, at mile post 4, a black tailed deer ran in front of their car. Bill, the driver, swerved to miss the deer and ran off the road, hitting a small Alder tree. It didn't do very much damage to the car, but they could not get it back on the road. So, Louie had to walk to his parent's house and get his father to bring his four-wheel drive truck to pull their vehicle back onto the road. This whole incident took several hours, and Louie's dad told Bill and Harley that Louie needed to get to bed as he needed him to work with him in the woods the next morning. So, that ended the school outhouse mischievous event by this notorious Scofield Gang.

Monday morning found the students and their teacher, Miss Ditto, back in school. At the morning recess the boys discovered that they could not get into their outhouse. Several of the older boys tried to dislodge the boards, but were not able to do so. They rushed into the school building and told Miss Ditto. She told the boys that they would have to use the girl's outhouse until she could get in touch with the school custodian. When Mrs. Brown stopped by for her daily visit, Miss Ditto asked her to contact the custodian and have him remove the boards.

The next morning, everything was taken care of, and the boys' outhouse was back in working order. Miss Ditto had a good idea of who had done the dirty work, but she could not prove it, and nothing was ever done about the incident.

Spring vacation started around the middle of April. The students were so excited to be free from school for a whole week. Fortunately, Louie's parents had planned on a family vacation to visit family in Kentucky. Bill spent the week with his parents at the beach near Tillamook, Oregon. With his 'partners in crime' gone for the week, Harley didn't cause any problems in either community.

The Tophill kids spent most of the week outdoors. The girls organized two or three dances at each other's homes. Again, not a single boy was invited. The older girls would liked to have invited some of the Scofield boys, but their parents would not allow that.

CHAPTER VIII

The Hunt for Chittum Bark

Most of the Tophill boys decided they would spend most everyday collecting Chittum bark. One of their uncles, Alf, agreed to take the bark to a buyer in Forest Grove. This bark is used by some of the pharmaceutical companies as one of the ingredients in a laxative, which is sold over the counter. So, every day after breakfast the boys would meet, and decide where to go in search of the Chittum trees. They normally did not have to go very far, as the trees were quite plentiful in certain areas. Each boy would bring a different item for lunch, and put everything in one big sack. They never worried about water, as there were many small creeks and springs in the area, to get drinking water from. Being country boys, they had learned a long time ago about how to use their hands for dipping water from a spring or creek.

By the middle of the week, they had collected over 50 pounds of bark, and at $.50 per pound they had earned $25.00. That was a lot of money. Of course, they had to wait for their money until Uncle Alf could take the bark to the buyer in Forest Grove.

On Thursday, Billy Riggle suggested they take the rest of the week off, and go fishing in a stream down in a canyon towards Buxton. They could reach the stream by walking down the railroad bed. All of the Top Hill cousins in the group thought that was an excellent idea. They were tired of scraping the Chittum bark from over 100 trees. Their hands were sore and callused from the hard work. There was only one problem with this whole idea of fishing. Not one boy owned a fishing pole. The group decided to hike down the tracks to Buxton and buy a fishing pole from Ray Freeman's store. Billy said, "I think I can borrow the money from my mother, but will you all agree that she needs to be paid back from the money we earned from the sale of the bark?" Everyone chimed in with a "Yes."

After borrowing $5.00 from his mother, Billy and the rest of the boys started for Buxton. It took about 2 hours to make the 5-mile trip. It only took a few minutes to pick out a pole and reel. Mr. Freeman put the line on the reel and helped the boys pick out some hooks, sinkers, spinners and a net. They only had enough money for one complete outfit. They were so excited, and in their excitement, they had forgot to pack a lunch. They were getting pretty hungry after the shopping spree. As they were about to head back to the railroad track, which would take them to the fishing hole, Melvin's dad pulled up in front of the store. The boys were very glad to see Uncle Charles. He gave them all the change he had in his pockets, which amounted to over $3.00. With the money they bought a lot of good stuff for lunch. They got to the fishing hole, which was at the bottom of a very deep canyon, about half way home, by around 1:00 p.m. As they descended down the steep bank Billy and George walked right into a bunch of stinging nettles. In just a few seconds their entire arms and hands were covered with little whelps, and did they ever sting. Fortunately, the other boys avoided that area. As usual, Chan caught the first fish. Before the afternoon was over the boys each caught at least one fish, so they had a nice catch to take home. Climbing back out of the canyon was quite a challenge, particularly to avoid the stinging nettles. But being country boys, they were certainly up to the challenge.

Scofield School and Play Shed

The boys needed to cross at least three long trestles on the journey home. They were crossing the last trestle, which crossed over the deepest canyon, when they heard a train approaching. Fortunately, there was a platform which extended out at least 10 feet from the tracks. It had a large barrel which was filled with water. The platform had side rails so the boys could circle around the barrel and be quite safe. As they awaited the train, Lee, the boy holding the plastic bag with the fish in it, accidentally dropped the bag, which ended up in the bottom of the canyon. Thankfully the Engineer saw the boys well in advance of reaching the trestle. He sounded the whistle and slowed the train down as much as possible. He waved at the boys as the engine passed the platform. He also gave them a big 'thumbs up.'

After the train passed, George, the oldest boy of the group said, "Lee since you dropped the bag with the fish in it, I think you should be the one to go down to the bottom of the canyon and retrieve the fish." Delbert agreed to go with Lee, so off they headed down the steep bank. They had only gone about 50 feet when they slid right into a big patch of stinging nettles. There were more screams of fright and pain. The duo finally got through the nettles and continued downward to the bottom. Fortunately, they spotted the bag with the fish and headed back up the steep bank, avoiding the area with the nettles. By the time they finished the climb, and joined the other boys, the sun had gone down and it was getting late. They had to hurry to get home before dark, but they made it. Their parents were happy to see them and really excited about the fish. Chan's mom agreed to have all the boys over the next night for a 'fish fry'. She looked at their whelps, and assured the boys that they would probably be gone my morning. Each boy went to his own home, after agreeing to get together in the morning to plan the last couple of days of their vacation from school. They agreed to meet at the small lookout tower on the hill above Aunt Alice's house at 9:00 a.m.

CHAPTER IX

The Purse In The Road Trick

Chan spoke up first. "Boys, I think it is about time for the 'purse in the road' trick, what do you guys think?" George was all for it but Melvin had some reservations. He reminded the boys that this trick is what angered one of the members of the gang that had been causing so much grief in both communities. Nevertheless, he agreed to participate, if that is what the others wanted to do. Lee and Delbert, the youngest members of the group, were excited to participate. They pretty much always went along with whatever the older boys wanted to do. George suggested they use one of his mother's old hand bags, and place an old billfold that his dad had discarded, inside. They decided to pull off this mischievous little act this afternoon, as long as it did not rain.

George collected the items to be used, and they all met behind the big stump, which was alongside the highway, near Grandpa Long's house. Chan said, "Boys, let's run for our lives when a car stops, we can meet at my house when everything is clear." The group sat quietly in anticipation of the first succor to stop his/her car. Three cars and one truck went by in the first 15 minutes. It was another 20 minutes before the next car came. The driver swerved a little bit to miss the bag, applied his brakes, and pulled to the side of the road. He got out of his car quickly and proceeded toward the middle of the road. George quickly pulled the bag to the side of the road, and the boys ran as fast as they could into the woods. The driver started yelling, using some very fowl words. He finally calmed down, got back in his car and drove off. Once the boys realized the coast was clear, they sat down and had a good laugh. It's a good thing that one of those cars that went by was not one of their parents.

With only three days left of their spring vacation from school, the Top Hill children were together most of the daylight hours, and well into the evening. The girls were planning a big dance party for Saturday evening. Some of the boys went fishing in a small stream below Grandpa Long's house. Duane suggested they construct a new raft out of some cedar logs, and spend part of the day on the pond behind his mother's house. They would catch salamanders and pollywogs. The old raft that his father had helped him build several years ago, had fallen to pieces. Most of the children loved the big pond, and many hours were spent there during their free time.

Lee and Delbert decided they wanted to go looking for grasshoppers up on the big hill behind Lee's house. They took fruit jars with lids to hold their captured hoppers. They completely forgot about Lee's mom's cow being pastured up there. This cow had a reputation of being very mean. They had only begun to catch the hoppers when they heard a noise. It sounded like something running very fast. Delbert looked up and yelled at Lee, "Lee, look what's coming toward us very fast." Lee said, "Drop the fruit jars, we need to head for the tower." Fortunately, several of the older boys in the community had a built a tower on the hill a few years ago. It was about 20' tall, with a ladder, which made it pretty easy to climb to the top. The tower had rail sides and benches. The tower was a great place to go and look at the night sky. Lee reached the tower first, with Delbert right behind him. The old mean cow was only a few yards back. They climbed to safety completely out of breath. The old cow just circled the tower, but she would not leave the area. Lee said, "Let's just set down and be real quiet and maybe she will give up and wander off to the far side of the hill. When she does, we will climb down and make a brake for the gate." The boys sat there for a least an hour, and finally the old mean cow left and went to another part of the pasture. Delbert said, "Ok Lee let's go, this is our opportunity to get down and back to safety." When Lee told his mom about what had happened, she said, "Alf, I told you we need to get rid of that darn cow."

CHAPTER X

The Vine Maple Forest

Saturday was the very last day the children were free to do whatever they wanted. Sunday was always church day, and visiting with relatives or friends from church. So, several of the boys and older girls made plans to spend the day at Tarzan's Jungle. This was a favorite place in the woods where there was about an acre of small Vine Maple trees. The boys, and sometimes the girls, would go there quite often. Climbing these vine-like trees made their arms and legs get stronger. The trees had no limbs, except at the very top, so the boys and girls had to pull themselves to the top using their arms and legs.

The game went something like this: Each boy or girl would pick the tree he/she wanted to start the game with. When the oldest boy said go, the entire group would start climbing. Upon reaching the top, the climbers would start swinging their tree back and forth. After a few swings the climber would grab hold of the next tree and start swinging it, letting go of the first tree. This would continue until the climber reached the far side of the grove. If a tree was not strong enough, and bent all the way to the ground, the climber had to go back to the starting tree and start all over. They usually only played this game on cool weather days.

Since this was the last 'free' day several boys and girls showed up. Duane was the oldest so it was up to him to organize the children for the game. There were several boys and a few girls that were really too small to climb the trees so Duane said, "We are going to have two age groups, let's give these little kids a chance to climb first." Lee protested, but it didn't do him any good. The little kids picked their tree and Duane said, "On three, start climbing. One, two, three!" No one made it more than about 6' off the ground on the first try. Duane said, "I'll give you a little demonstration of how it's best to climb." With that, he grabbed hold of a tree and was to the top in just a few minutes. The little kids all chimed in together and said, "We can do that, can we have another try?" Duane said, "Sure," so they all went to their favorite tree and waited for Duane to tell them to start climbing. With this new climbing technique most of the boys, and a few girls, made it almost half way up, but not far enough to be able to make the trees start swinging back and forth. So, they all descended to the bottom and decided they would just watch the older children.

The results of the older children's climb were quite different from the last time they climbed these trees. George came in first, Duane second, and Melvin last. Alice Louise and Jeannie came in first for the girls. They had a great time. Duane had brought a new package of Oreo cookies, which he shared with everyone. After the competition the boys spent some time just climbing the trees and swinging just for fun. The girls had had enough climbing for the day, and their legs had scratches and bruises all over. Girls in those days always wore dresses. Most of the little guys were too tired to do any more climbing. It was almost supper time, time to head for home. Delbert said, "Duane, when can we do this again?" Duane's reply was, "Maybe next Saturday."

Monday morning found all of the school age children back in school. They were all very happy to see one another. Miss Ditto had a hard time getting them to settle down. She knew they all had a lot to talk about so she gave them an extra recess the first day back. The first thing the older boys did was to look around the school grounds to see if there was any damage done to their play equipment by the gang members, during spring break. Fortunately, everything appeared to be just like it was prior to the spring vacation.

CHAPTER XI

More Mean Pranks At Tophill By The Gang

Louie, Bill and Harley were also back from their vacations, and wasted no time in plotting their next mischievous event. Bill said, "Louie, did you come up with any bright ideas of ways we could have some 'real fun' in our community and Top Hill?" Bill, the youngest member of the gang, said, "You know, as I was driving through Top Hill on my way to Vernonia the other day, I noticed the family that lives in the house who had that mean dog that took a chunk out of Louie's leg, has a large chicken coup and fenced in area for their chickens. Why don't we just go by there late some night and cut a nice big hole in fence?" Louie spoke up and said, "Bill, why don't you drive by again and see if you can spot any other chicken runs? They have to be pretty close to the road, so we don't get caught. Let's meet back at my house in a week and make a plan." Harley spoke up and said, "My dad has several wire cutters in his shop, so I will furnish them for our little project."

The gang met as planned at Louie's house and decided the best night for their next little destructive act would be Wednesday night of next week. Bill informed the group that he had spotted two more places with chicken runs near the road. Louie said, "What time and where should we meet on Wednesday? We can go in my car." They all agreed to meet at 10 p.m. at the rail road track crossing near Bill's house.

Louie arrived first and suggested that Bill and Harley leave their cars at home. After the two gang members dropped their cars off, Louie picked them up and headed for Top Hill. When they arrived at State Highway 47 junction and Scofield Road, Bill suggested they do the chicken run that was about one fourth mile down the highway towards Vernonia, first. Louie drove by slowly, with his head lights turned off, hoping not to pass an oncoming car. They parked on the opposite side of the road of the chicken coop. There was a crescent moon, so they had no trouble seeing. Louie took his wire cutters, and the trio headed for the chicken run. They moved quickly and quietly. It only took a few minutes to cut a good-sized hole in the chicken wire. They hurried back to the car and drove to the house near the intersection of Scofield Road. There were two or three houses in the immediate area, so they had to be really careful, making sure there were no lights on in either house. Louie parked the car about one block down the gravel road, and they walked back to the chicken run.

Harley said, "Louie, I get the pleasure of doing this one." He grabbed the wire cutters out of Louie's hands. Just as he applied the cutters to the first strand of wire, Bill yelled, "Look out guys, the back door to the house opened, and I see that horrible mean dog coming toward us at full speed." Harley tried to remove the cutters from the wire but he could not free them, so he let go of the handles, and the boys ran for their lives. Just as Louie opened the door, the dog grabbed his pant leg, and in the process took another chunk out of the same leg that was bitten before on their last visit to this place. Louie was in too much pain to drive, and he was also bleeding quite profusely. It was quite late when the boys got back to Harley's house. He and Bill helped Louie clean and dress his wound. Louie was ok to drive by then, so he took Bill home. So, again their mean little mischievous act didn't turn out so well.

When Oscar went out the next morning to feed his chickens, he got quite a surprise when he found an almost new set of wire cutters hanging from a wire on his chicken run. He knew then why his dog took off running for the road when he let him out last night.

Later that morning, my dad went over to tell his brother, Oscar, that someone had cut a hole in our chicken run last night, and that all of his chickens were out in our front yard when he got up. Oscar said, "I'll go and help repair your chicken run, and then we can put the chickens back inside." Within an hour, the fence was repaired and the chickens were back inside. Oscar said, "Charles, do you think we should report this to the Sheriff's office?" Charles said, "No, it probably wouldn't do any good. They have more important things to do with all the recent burglaries that seem to be taking place in the county. Also, I read in this morning's paper where folks who leave their cars outside are finding their gas tanks empty. With gas being rationed it is no wonder. I am fortunate because I get extra ration stamps because of my church calling."

When I got up my dad told me what had happened. I said, "Dad, it looks like those ruffians from Scofield have been at it again." Dad said, "Now son, you don't know that they did it, don't be so quick to accuse anyone at this time. Besides, you Uncle Oscar got a new set of expensive wire cutters that he found hanging on a wire in his run." I never heard anything more about the chicken run incident.

The days were getting warmer so the children were able to spend more time outside during recess. Occasionally, Miss Ditto even came outside to observe her students. She was always careful to offer words of encouragement to the younger students who seemed afraid of the older boys. She made sure they got their fair share of the small playing field. Most of the girls preferred to play inside the play shed. Dodge ball and four square were popular games being played at that time. Oftentimes, Joe and Hyrum, my uncles, found pleasure in picking up a garden snake and chasing their girl nieces. The Top Hill boys and the Scofield boys almost always got along very well.

April usually meant warmer and longer days. Miss Ditto always gave us a little longer recess. The boys started bringing their softball mitts to school and the girls their jump ropes. Of course, there was always Dodge Ball and other games that could be played in the large covered play shed, rain or shine. I well remember one particular afternoon about the middle of April. We had just returned to our desks when the neighbor lady, Mrs. Fellas, came into the, room and went directly to Miss Ditto's desk. She asked Miss Ditto if she could talk to her out in the coat and hat room. When Miss Ditto came back in the class room, she had tears in her eyes. She told us that the President of The United States, President Roosevelt had died. That didn't seem to register with the primary grade children, but some of the older children started to cry. Miss Ditto was very somber for the rest of the day. She did tell us that the Vice President, Harry S. Truman, would be sworn in as President, to finish out Roosevelt's fourth term in office.

CHAPTER XII

The Softball Game

About the first of May, some of the Scofield parents decided that Scofield School should have a softball team. They approached Miss Ditto with the idea. She was all for it, but assured the parents that she would not be able to help out. Mr. Berge spoke up and offered to organize and coach the team. There were just enough boys and girls in the upper grades to make a team of nine players. Mr. Berge came during the afternoon recess every day, when it was not raining, and worked with the team. Finally, he felt they were ready for their first game. He invited the coach of the Buxton Grade School team to bring his team to Scofield for the first game. And what a game it turned out to be, with the Scofield winning the game by a score of 9 to 8. Toby Birch was the star of the game, hitting three home runs. Duane pitched for five innings and then Mr. Berge brought in his son, John, who pitched the last four innings. The two teams agreed to meet the following week in Buxton.

Most of the folks in the Scofield community, and a few from Tophill came to support their team. I noticed that all three of the Scofield Ruffians were there with their parents. I saw Louie whisper something to Harley and Bill, when he overhead Mr. Berge and the coach from Buxton agree to play the next game in Buxton on the following Friday.

The sun was just coming up when I awakened Saturday morning. I wanted to get my cow milking chore out of the way early, as my cousin, Duane, said he would go with all of us boys to Tarzan's Jungle. My family and I had just sat down for breakfast when Duane knocked on our door. I invited him in and dad asked if he had had breakfast. He said, "No, Uncle Charley, and I am really hungry." Mom fixed him a plate of food and I poured him a large glass of milk. Duane said that he had sent his brother, George, to roundup all the other boys. He was told to meet us at the jungle at 9:00 a.m.

What a morning it turned out to be. We had several races across the jungle. Duane made sure that all the younger boys got to climb. We were all very tired and thirsty within a couple of hours. I invited everyone to my house to have a glazed doughnut. My Grandpa Bailey had given us 2 dozen doughnuts the day before.

Monday morning found the students in both communities back in school. Miss Ditto rang the bell at 9:00 a.m. sharp, as usual. As soon as we were all in our seats and quiet, she said, "I have some sad news to tell you. Someone broke into the school over the weekend and stole all of our softball equipment; the bats, balls, mitts and even the make shift bases. There is no money in the budget to replace these things so I must tell you, we will not be able to play the game on Friday with Buxton. I will try to put money in the budget for next year, but that will not help now."

Immediately, I heard the boys whispering back and forth. I raised my hand and said, "I bet I know who did it. It's probably the same ones that wired our school doors shut." Miss Ditto said, "Now Melvin, we mustn't accuse someone unless we know for sure."

With that, the boys and girls started raising their hands to be recognized. Huey was recognized first. He said, "Teacher I have a new soft ball that my dad just gave me for my birthday. I will be happy to bring it to school." Another boy offered to bring his two bats to school. Several of the boys offered to bring their mitts for practice and the game. Bruce Berge said he was sure that he could bring several mitts and balls. Before long we had more than enough equipment for practice and the game. Miss Ditto said, "All right boys and girls, the game is on. That's enough about softball, we must begin our studies for the day."

Mr. Berge came and practiced with our team every noon recess during the week. We all felt pretty good about our team, and the chances of again beating the Buxton team. Game day, Friday, finally arrived. Miss Ditto had asked three or four of our parents to transport us to Buxton, and then deliver team members to their homes after the game. The drivers were, Mrs. Berge, my Aunt Alice, and Mrs. Attwood. Several parents from all three communities showed up for the game. Miss Ditto and the principal from Buxton agreed to let school out right after the lunch break. As soon as we got to the school, I saw all three of the Scofield ruffians in the stands with their parents. I tried not to look at them, but each time I did, I Louie would give me a real mean look. Before the game started, I needed to go to the restroom. When I came out of the men's toilet Louie was getting ready to go in. He purposely put his foot out and tripped me. I got up quickly, dusted myself off, and joined my team. I never said a word to anyone about the incident. I just wanted to get on with the game.

John Berge started pitching for Scofield and Duane Ross started for Buxton. Scofield only had 9 players so everyone got to play the entire game. I played left field. Duane pitched the last two innings for Scofield, and one of the Bigsbee boys pitched the last two innings for Buxton. We had two girls on our team, my cousin Alice Louise and my sister Reva. The principals from both schools agreed to be fair, Buxton would also have to play two girls.

The game went something like this:
First inning: Scofield 0 Buxton 0
Second inning: Scofield 1 Buxton 1
Third inning: Scofield 2 Buxton 1

Fourth inning: Scofield 1 Buxton 2
Fifth inning: Scofield 0 Buxton 1
Sixth inning: Scofield 1 Buxton 0

Seventh inning and what was supposed to be the final inning: Scofield 1 Buxton 1.

At that point the coaches talked and decided that they would play one more inning to see if the tie could be broken. Both teams were very happy to play another inning. The eighth inning was so exciting. Scofield was up first. Bernard Stanfill grounded out with a hit right to the pitcher. Bobby Berge hit a fly ball to center field. Things were not looking good for Scofield. My cousin George hit a double. The next batter, Toby Birch came to the plate. The pitcher got two strikes on him right away. The third pitch came right over the plate and Toby swung with all his might. The ball went clear over the center fielder's head for a home run. That gave Scofield two runs. The next batter, my cousin, Chan, grounded out to the third base, which ended the inning for Scofield.

Buxton came to the plate. The first batter up, Duane Ross, hit a home run. That made the score: Scofield 8 Buxton 7. The next batter hit a fly ball to the center fielder. The third batter hit a ground ball to second base but the second baseman overthrew at first, so the batter was safe. The batter advanced to second base on a wild pitch. The next batter grounded out to the third baseman. That meant there were now two outs. The next batter was a Bigsbee boy. He was supposed to be their best overall hitter. On the first pitch, he hit a long fly ball directly to me in left field. I said a quick prayer when I saw the ball coming my way. Everyone in the stands rose to see if I would catch the ball. My Aunt Alice later told me that she held her breath and also said a quick prayer. A miracle happened and I caught the ball. That ended the game with the score: Scofield 8 Buxton 7. Everyone on my team ran to me and carried me all the way to our bench. The Buxton team members were such good sports as was our team members. We all congratulated each other. After the game Mrs. Berge had popsicles for everyone on both teams. We had so much fun. We all thanked Miss Ditto for allowing us to play both games. She even attended the game in Buxton, as she was on her way home to Banks. All of the Tophill players rode home with Aunt Alice. I could hardly wait to get home to tell my parents about the game. When Aunt Alice let me out before going up her drive way, as usual, I first went to my Grandma Bailey's house to tell grandma and grandpa about the game. Grandpa didn't say much, but grandma gave me a big hug. Of course, the real reason I went to their house first was to get a slice of bread with peanut butter and honey on it. Grandpa came into the kitchen and brought out a bottle of Hires root beer. Using his little tin cup, he gave me and Reva some root beer. We thanked him and then rushed off to our home across the street.

Those were the only two soft ball games we played with another school that year, but oh what fun! Who would have dreamed that we could beat a big school like Buxton?

CHAPTER XIII
───────────
Summer Vacation

The last day of school was always so much. Miss Ditto always drove her car, a very nice-looking Studebaker. We had classes in the morning. We then turned in our text books so they could be stored on the shelves for next year. We put everything else in our desk in a sack to be taken home for the summer. Miss Ditto brought ice cream, punch and cookies of all kinds, for everyone. I think some of the parents also brought goodies. Parents were invited, as it was necessary to take their children home after the party. It was pretty much a community affair. The three Scofield ruffians never missed an opportunity for free food, and yes, they showed up. However, Miss Ditto promptly told the boys they were not welcome, and she escorted them out the gate. This might have been a mistake, because it could have given them more determination to continue with their little pranks during the summer.

    I later learned that Miss Ditto made a visit to the parents of all three troublemakers and put them on notice: She told the parents that she would be making a trip to the school once each week during the summer, and if she found any damage on the school building or the school grounds, she would file a complaint with the Sheriff's office immediately. These boys were well known by the State Police and County Sheriff.

    We were all very happy to be out of school. As far as I know everyone was promoted to the next higher grade. Miss Ditto always had a nice graduation program for the eighth graders, in the evening of the last day of school, but I never got to attend. You will see why latter in the book.

Spring came early this year, so that also meant strawberry picking started earlier than normal. All of the Tophill children, over the age of 5 or 6, were expected to pick strawberries, and in some cases beans. I started picking berries when I was 5 years old and I picked, along with three of my siblings, every summer. All of my cousins, and some of my father's younger brothers, also picked berries. We all picked for the same grower, a Mr. Al Davies of Banks, Oregon. Most of the time he would come to Top Hill and pick us up in his large flatbed truck. We all loved to be together in the berry fields. Some of the time our parents and grandparents would come with us to pick berries. Our Grandma Long was a good berry picker. She was amazing, in that she could carry a carrier in each hand and put one of top of her head, and take them to the check-in person. We got paid about .30 cents per carrier. A real good picker could make $10 to $12 on a good day. Most of the berry pickers were local kids from all the little communities in our part of the county. There were also families that came from Oklahoma and Missouri. They were good, hardworking families. They were called Okies. Berry season usually lasted for three or four weeks. When we got home from picking for Al Davies, oft times we would go down to our neighbor, Tracy Everett's place, and pick her strawberries. The money we made there we got to keep. She would always pay us in cash each night.

This turned out to be a great summer. The ruffians from Scofield got summer jobs planting trees in the Tillamook Burn area for the State Forest Service, so they were gone all summer.

We had so much fun being together all summer long. The younger girls, like Rita, Jeannie, Ida, Marjorie, Mary Linda, Sandy, Linda and Wilma would spend hours catching pollywogs and salamanders in nearby ponds. The older girls were always planning dancing parties at one of their homes. All of us would meet most evenings and play games, such as softball, run sheep run, kick the can, or hide and seek. We ended the day with a bonfire. We hardly ever got home before 9:30 or 10:00 p.m.

Aunt Alice would take her bunch bean picking most summers. My mom did not drive, and dad was always working, so we missed the bean picking, thank goodness.

We also spent a lot of time climbing the vine maple trees in Tarzan's Jungle. The amazing thing about swinging from those trees is that no one ever had a serious fall or broke any bones. There were times when the boys wanted the jungle all to themselves. This was a challenge because, it seems as though there would always be one girl that would see us trying to sneak away. She would tell the other girls. Sometimes, they would not bother to come, so we would have the jungle to ourselves.

One afternoon a neighbor lady, Mrs. Helms, came to our house and told my dad that she was worried about her husband. He had gone across the road into the woods to go fishing in the small creek nearby. He had been gone for several hours. She also told dad that he was diabetic. Dad told her that he would have his brother-in-law Alf come over, and the two of them would look for her husband. They spent several hours looking for Dudley, and finally, they found him about a mile from his house. He had evidently had a diabetic seizure, and had fallen face down into the creek and drowned. This was a tragedy and a sad time for our community. My dad and Uncle Alf carried the sad news to Mrs. Helms.

CHAPTER XIV

The County Sheriff Calls At Our House

One Saturday afternoon I heard a knock on our front door. When I answered the door, a County Sheriff introduced himself. He said, "Young man, is your father home?" I said, "Sure, I will get him." Dad came to the door and invited the sheriff in. Dad said, "What can I help you with?" The sheriff introduced himself as Officer Barnes. Dad also introduced himself. The sheriff said, "Mr. Long, how well do you know your neighbor, Mr. Christensen?" Dad said, "Pretty well, even though he really hasn't lived in our community that long. He works with dynamite, and I have had him blow several stumps to clear away an area for our garden. He seems to be very friendly and always willing to help out if I need him." Sheriff Barnes said, "Very good, there is a situation going on at their home right now that is very tense. Mr. Christensen is threatening to blow up the entire family. Mrs. Christensen called the Sheriff's Office and I was in the vicinity and responded to the call. When I approached the house, Mr. Christensen came to the door and said if I came any closer, he would ignite the fuse to the dynamite. I backed off immediately and came to your house. Mr. Long, would you be willing to go to their home and see if you can talk to Mr. Christensen and get him calmed down?" Dad said, "Did it appear that he was drunk?" Sheriff Barnes said, "No. I can spot a drunk when I see one or hear him speak."

Dad said, "Sure, I'll go talk to Lloyd, but I think you should stay in your car a little distance away. I'll walk up there and see if I can calm him down." Sheriff Barnes said, "Are you sure you would be willing to do this? I don't want you to put yourself in harm's way." Dad said, "Sheriff, if I had any doubts, or if I was the least bit worried, I wouldn't do this. I know Lloyd and our families are pretty close, you have to be close to your neighbors living out here in the sticks as we do." Sheriff Barnes said, "You are right about that, Mr. Long."

I asked Dad if I could go with him, but he said, "No, son, you best stay home with your mom and the rest of the children. This is something I better do alone." Sheriff Barnes got back in his car and drove about half way between our house and the Christensen's. It was only about a five-minute walk for dad. He came back in about half an hour. He had stopped on the way and told Sheriff Barnes that everything was okay. Lloyd had calmed down, and that there was no need for him to go back to the house, it would just make matters worse. Dad told the sheriff that he would visit with Lloyd every day for the next week, and see if he could get him to open up and tell him what was bothering him. Dad is also going to invite the family down for Sunday dinner. My dad has a lot of experiences dealing with family situations, as he is the leader of our Branch of the church. Sheriff Barnes asked dad to call him next week with an update on the family situation. Sheriff Barnes thanked my father, and said that he would make a full report to the County Sheriff. In all of the rest of the years that the family lived next to us, there was never another situation like this, thank goodness.

CHAPTER XV

The Unauthorized Use Of My Uncle's Car

One afternoon, my cousin, Alice Louise, came to me and said, "Why don't we take my dad's car and go over to the school, so we can play on the playground? We can invite a bunch of our cousins and other friends to go along with us." By the time everyone showed up, we had 10 kids who wanted to go. The car was a 1931 Model A Ford sedan, which normally seats no more than 5 people. We managed to get 6 people inside, and we had two standing on the running board on each side of the car. With everyone on board we headed for Scofield School. We took the car without asking my Uncle Oscar's permission. None of our parents were aware of this little adventure. We had only gone a little way when I realized that we did not have any brakes, other than the emergency brake. That did not stop us, as we knew we would not be traveling very fast. The trip was going well, until we had to make a 90 degree turn from the road we were on to the road that led to the school. So, when I turned the corner, not being able to slow down, as I could not reach the emergency brake, all four of the kids riding on the fenders flew off. The car nearly tipped over, as it was difficult to bring it under control. One girl, Velma Radar, landed face down on the gravel road, and was knocked unconscious. She had several small cuts and scratches. We got her into the car quickly, and her brother, Marvin, started slapping her lightly on her cheeks to bring her back. She did recover pretty quickly. We were all very scared. I managed to turn the car around and we drove back to Tophill. We managed to get Velma cleaned up without any of our parents ever finding out about our little accident.

I have driven by that site many times since, and I am always reminded of the incident. I think we were very fortunate that the car did not tip over on its side and that no one was seriously injured. I think we all learned a lesson that day.

**

My brother, Delbert, had been suffering from a tooth ache for a while. Finally, dad gave him $5.00 and told him to walk over to Dr. Brown's place in Scofield, and have him pull the tooth. Dr. Brown had closed his practice in Hillsboro, and was practicing dentistry at his home. Delbert and our cousin, Lee, were very close, so Delbert went to his house and asked if he would walk over to Dr. Brown's place, as he needed to get a tooth pulled. Lee said, "Sure, let me check with mom to see if she is ok with me going with you." When the boys got to Dr. Brown's place, they found him working out in his barn. He told them to go to his house and have Mrs. Brown get things prepared, and that he would be there in a few minutes to examine Delbert's tooth. When he arrived at the house, he took off his boots, washed his hands, and proceeded to examine Delbert's tooth. Dr. Brown said, "Young man, I think this tooth is too far gone to save. The only thing I can do to help you is to remove the tooth." Delbert said, "Well, Dr. Brown, that's what my dad said to have you do." So, into Delbert's gums went the Novocaine and about 15 minutes later, out came the infected tooth. All the while that Delbert was in the dentist chair, Lee was in the living room flirting with the Brown twins, Agnes and Fayne, who were in the same grade as him.

With Delbert's tooth removed, and enough Novocaine to keep the pain under control for perhaps 30 minutes, the boys started for home, a distance of about three miles. When they got to the intersection of Scofield Road and Nowaskoski Road, the Gamroth boys were waiting for them. Evidently, Lee knew these boys were trouble. Lee told Delbert to run, as he knew he was in no condition to fight. Delbert only went a short distance, and then turned around to see how the fight was going. (Let me say at this point in my story, there is a little difference in how the fight went, depending who is telling the story. I will only give Lee's version, as he is the one that was directly involved in the fight.) Lee said to the Gamroth boys, "Come on you two, let's get it on." With that, the oldest boy came at Lee. Lee grabbed him by one arm and threw him into the blackberry vines. The younger boy then came at him. Lee grabbed him by the arm and threw him into the blackberry vines on top of his brother. By the time the Gamroth boys worked themselves out of the vines, Lee and Delbert were well on their way to Tophill.

**

By the end of August, most of the summer crops were harvested, and we were all thinking about going back to school. So, it was time to start shopping for 'back to school clothes'. For our family, that usually meant at least one trip to the huge Montgomery Ward Store in Portland. Dad always took us directly to the bargain floor. My brothers and I would get a new pair of Levis, a couple of shirts, socks and some under clothes. The younger girls would get a new dress each and the older girls would get new skirts and blouses. We never bought shoes there. After shopping, Dad always insisted we go visit his Aunt Ada in St. Johns, a suburb of Portland. I don't remember being very excited about those visits. The next shopping trip was to the J.C. Penney Store in Forest Grove. We always got one new pair of shoes, which was expected to last throughout the school year. About half way through the year, the soles and heels would wear out. When that happened, our dear Grandpa Bailey would get his shoe repair equipment out, and we would go home with new soles and heels on our shoes. Most of the time the boys and girls would also get one pair of rubber boots to be worn during the cold and wet winter months.

Summer was a great time to enjoy vegetables from our Grandpa Bailey's Garden. He planted a big garden every summer and he was always willing to share what was being harvested. He would also come to our place and plow up a small area for our garden, but I can only remember dad planting, green onions, a little lettuce, and some peas. Grandpa always planted pumpkins so we could carve Jack-O-Lanterns for Halloween.

School always started the day after Labor Day. So, Tuesday morning, September the 4th of 1945 found all of the school age children waiting patiently for the big yellow bus to arrive. I was excited because my little sister, Jeannie was in the first grade. She had been wanting to go to school for the last couple of years. The children were particularly happy this day, as just two days prior, on September 2, there was much celebration in their little community of Top Hill, as they had learned of the surrender of the Japanese, ending WWII. This meant that Uncle Lawrence and Uncle Hobert would be coming home soon.

Miss Ditto greeted each child as he/she got on the bus. She always sat in the same seat every day: the second seat back on the right side of the bus. She seemed also to be in a very happy mood. Miss Ditto said she would give us an extra 15 minutes before ringing the bell to begin the school day. She knew we had a lot to talk about with all of our Scofield friends. The older kids talked about the war ending. The younger children were so happy to see their young friends, they knew very little about the war. Almost every family had an uncle or relative that would be coming home soon. Unfortunately, one or two families had lost loved ones in the war effort. The end of the war also meant the end of rationing soon. This made everyone happy.

The bell rang and everyone rushed inside to see where they would be setting. Miss Ditto welcomed everyone back to school. She started by saying, "Boys and girls, the first thing we need to do, is what we do every year on the first day back. So, let's have everyone line up by grade. The first graders in the front row, second grades next and so on. If there is ever a fire, we need to be able to get out of the building as quickly and safely as possible." In just a few minutes, everyone was lined up properly. I was reminded of the time I was in first grade, and the terrible events of that day.

After the fire drill, Miss Ditto asked a girl from the 7th grade and a boy from the 8th grade to take the three first grades out and show them where the toilets were located and to give them a tour of the school grounds. This was always a big honor each year to be given this assignment. There were 29 students in all eight grades. There was also a new family that moved into the Scofield community, by the name of Cartwright. More about this family later in the story. We were all excited to get home that first day back, and tell our parents how happy we were to be back in school with our friends from Scofield. There was also a new family that lived near our community, by the name of Yost, but their children were older, so they rode the bus on to Banks.

We learned that the three ruffians, Bill, Harley, and Louie, were still working for the State Forest Service, planting trees in the Tillamook Burn area. We were told by Bill's sister, Cathrine, that they probably would not return until the snow season came.

We were all excited for Sunday to come, to be able to go to church at our little Branch of the LDS Church, in Vernonia. My Aunt Alice took us to Primary a couple of times during the summer. My dad told us that there was a new large family with 11 children that had moved into our

Branch, by the name of Rice. They had moved to Vernonia from Utah. We were excited to have so many new children in the Branch. This would also enlarge the Branch Primary. More about the Rice family later on.

My dad and several of his brothers, and our Uncle Alf, were still working at the large sawmill in Vernonia. Life in general got a lot better for every family, now that the war was over. Most of the things that were rationed became more readily available, with the end of rationing. With men returning home from the service, many of the mothers who had taken jobs that needed to be filled, were now able to return home and be full time mothers and housewives. All of the Top Hill kids were anxiously waiting for their Uncles Larry and Hobert to return home.

CHAPTER XVI

The Three Ruffians Strike At Tophill Again

Winter came early in our part of Oregon, and with that came the return of the three ruffians, Harley, Bill, and Louie. Bill invited Harley and Louie to go with him to a movie. After the movie Bill said, "Boys, I have an idea of how we can get gas for our vehicles without buying it." After hearing Bill's idea, they wasted no time in resuming their old truant ways of mischief in both neighborhoods. Being unemployed now, they decided to engage in steeling gasoline from neighbors' cars. In those days, it was a fairly easy process. There were no locking gas caps, so all one had to do was get a rubber hose and siphon gasoline from the car's tank. Very few people had garages so vehicles were an easy target. The first family in Top Hill to have missing gas was my Uncle Harvey. He reported the theft to the County Sheriff, but was told there was nothing much they could do unless he could positively identify the culprits. Our Top Hill parents started parking their cars as close to their houses as possible. This seemed to help a little bit for a couple of weeks. The next family at Top Hill to have gas taken from their car was Ed Everett. Again, he contacted the Sheriff's Office, and was given the same answer as my Uncle Harvey.

The gas stealing went on, unabated, for about three weeks. Uncle Ed, whose house was very close to the road, was the next Top Hill resident to have his gas tank emptied. Finally, my father Charles, called all of his brothers to come to our house to see if someone could come up with a plan to catch these gas thieves. Uncle Oscar came up with an idea. He suggested that on a given week he would remove the gas tank from his Model A and replace it with an old one. He would then fill the tank with a mixture of gasoline and water. He would leave the car setting outside and not drive it that week. Dad said that he would let Oscar use one of our vehicles that week. All agreed that this was a good plan. On Saturday afternoon, Dad helped Oscar with removing the good tank and replacing it with an old tank. They took five-gallon buckets and filled the tank with water and gasoline.

Uncle Oscar decided that he would stay up late Saturday night to see if the gas thieves would show up. He turned all the lights out and sat by the kitchen window, with a clear view of his Model A. It was a full moon so he knew he would be able to see anyone that approached his car. About 11:30 pm, the Scofield Gang showed up. Each one had what looked to be a two-gallon can. Louie had a siphon hose so he started the process of filling his can first. Within 20 minutes, they had their cans full and were on their way. Louie emptied the first 2-gallon can of stolen gas into his vehicle when he got home. Harley emptied the second two-gallon can of stolen gas into his car when he got home. Bill emptied his can of stolen gas into his car the next morning. Neither car would start the next morning. The gang never again stole gas from the Tophill families. I am sure the gang went on to other communities like Buxton and Manning. After leaving his Model A out near the road for a week, my dad helped Uncle Oscar remove the old tank and put the good tank back on. Dad also gave Oscar a can of gas and some money to fill his tank.

With fall came Halloween, and much colder weather. We all wondered if the Scofield Gang would pay a visit to Top Hill or if they had learned their lesson from the last Halloween? As it turned out, most of the mischief that took place was done by the Long boys themselves. The younger children, like me many others, were able to have a great time going from house to house. Our favorite house to go to was Tracy and Ed Everett's. They always had us come in to enjoy hot chocolate and home-made cookies. Grandma and Grandpa Bailey always gave out a glazed doughnut and sometimes an apple. Grandpa and Grandma Long always gave us each an apple.

Our fathers and Grandpa Long continued to work at the large sawmill in Vernonia. Our little Branch of the Church was such a big part of our lives. My father, Charles, was serving as the Branch President. There were a few new families that moved into the Branch, and we were blessed to have full time missionaries, Sister Hart and Sister Henderson.

In early December Anne Rice told my father that she and her husband needed to make a trip back to Utah to settle some business affairs. They could not find anyone to watch the children so, my dad volunteered he and Mom's services. Uncle Ed and Alice Marie lived in a little one room shanty next to our house and they agreed to look after us children. The Rice family were very, very poor. When they left for Utah, there was no food in the house. Dad and Mom went to Safeway's in Vernonia and bought groceries to last for several days. My dad had such a big heart, and he was more than willing to do whatever needed to be done for anyone in his congregation. He was loved by those he served. The Rice's returned in about a week and we were so happy to have our parents back home.

CHAPTER XVII
The Gang Of Three Continue Their Pranks At The School

Photo of miniature model of Scofield School built by Dick Minor.
Front view of model built by Dick Minor

December brought colder weather and snow to the area. The children were looking forward to Christmas and a vacation from school. The school Christmas party was held on Friday evening December 21st. It had snowed about six inches during the day. The parents parked their cars along the road side in front of the school, as they always did, as there was no parking lot on the school grounds. This gave Louie, Bill, and Harley a perfect opportunity to continue their mischievous ways. This time it was Louie's idea they pursued. Louie said, "Bill, Harley, let's have some fun." Harley said, "Tell us more." Louie said, "Let's put the blade on my old jeep and go plow the snow off the road so that the parents will have difficulty getting their cars out over the bank of snow, after the Christmas program." Bill and Harley thought this is was a great idea. They both told Louie that neither of their parents planned to attend the program, as neither of their parents had children in school any longer. Louie went to their barn and got his old jeep out. With the help of his friends, they had the blade on in short order. They all three piled in and off they went. They made several passes on the road, always plowing the snow in the direction of the parked cars.

Our Christmas program was always very special. Every student got to play a part in the Nativity. There were Wise Men, Angels, Shepherds, Mary and Joseph, and of course Baby Jesus. The program ended with a special visitor, Santa Claus. He always gave out popcorn balls and oranges. When the program was over, everyone got a big surprise when they went to their cars to go home. They found about two feet of snow between their cars and the road. My Aunt Alice is the only one who had a shovel in the trunk of her car. Alf got it out and several of the men started shoveling. Each dad had his family go back into the school to wait where it was warm. Miss Ditto was really upset and said she would try to find out who did this dastardly deed. Aunt Alice spoke up and said, "Miss Ditto, we all are pretty sure we know who the culprits are." To my knowledge, no one was ever punished for this mischievous act.

Christmas was a wonderful time for the families in both communities. One afternoon, several of us went down to Tracy Everett's place to take her and Ed some caramel popcorn balls. Tracy was glad to see us. She apologized for not making it to our Christmas program at school. We told her what happened, and that it was a good thing that she didn't go. She invited us in and said that she had something she thought we might like trying to do. She had Ed get out an old pair of wooden skies with poles. Ed got some wax out and rubbed it on the bottom of the skis. Ed said he would go with us to a hill behind their house and teach us how to ski. Boy did we have fun. I think we spent more time getting up after falling, but eventually everyone made one trip down the hill without falling. Afterwards, Tracy had us come in their house where she gave us hot chocolate and cookies. We were all very tired when we got home.

We always looked forward to our Branch Church Christmas program and dinner. Our Vernonia Branch was like one big family. There were probably 50 or 60 active members in the Branch. We were not in a Church Stake, but part of the Northwestern States Mission, and the McMinnville District.

It snowed almost every day of the Christmas vacation. On Christmas Eve my siblings and I always left a snack for Santa on the living room table. As we got a little older, we learned that it was our dear Grandpa Bailey that brought a sack full of toys and gifts that Grandma Bailey purchased or made during the year. We always had a wonderful Christmas. My siblings and I would visit our dear Grandma Bailey almost every day during the vacation. I have fond memories of setting on her lap, as she sat in her comfortable rocking chair. Sometimes, she would tell us stories about her life as a little girl, growing up in South Africa and Holland. Once in a while, we could get a word or two out of grandpa about his sheep herding days in the Wallowa Mountains of Eastern Oregon. Grandma also told us about how she immigrated to the United States from Holland when she was a young woman, leaving her family and friends to come to America.

Because of the snow and cold weather, the Scofield ruffians did not cause us any trouble during the vacation at Tophill. I did hear of one incident that happened in Scofield. Louie decided that it would be fun to pile snow on the road where it crossed the train tracks, the same spot where they had attempted, but failed with their little switch escapade. Wayne Atwood told me about the incident when I saw him and his mom at Score's Store in Buxton one evening. Evidently Louie and his gang members took his jeep, with the blade on the front, pushed snow onto the crossing until it was several feet deep. By doing so they hoped to make it difficult, if not impossible, for cars to make it across the tracks. Again, their little mischievous prank did not turn out as they had hoped. The train came through the next morning, had a blade on in front, and removed the snow completely. Mr. Atwood, who lived nearby, arrived shortly thereafter and shoveled the rest of the snow away so cars could pass through without any problem.

January 1948 through August of 1950

By the end of the Christmas vacation, we were all anxious to get back to school, mainly to see our Scofield friends. It was always exciting to learn what others got for Christmas. Miss Ditto always gave us extra time for the morning recess to share with our friends about our vacation. Many of the students brought some of their presents to school. The younger girls brought dolls and the older girls brought make-up kits. The younger boys brought cap guns and cowboy outfits while the older boys brought new softball mitts, and bats. Everyone had at least one piece of clothes on that he/she received for Christmas. Lunch pails were full of Christmas candy, oranges, apples and other goodies.

CHAPTER XVIII

Fun On The Ice Ruined By The Ruffians

The weather turned very cold so Miss Ditto reminded everyone to dress extra warm or they would not be able to go outside for recess. The snow continued to pile up. By the end of the second week of January it stopped snowing and the skies cleared up, but the temperature never got about 30 degrees Fahrenheit. The hill on the north side of the school building turned to ice. This what we all had been waiting for. Some of the boys brought gunnysacks, others brought old discarded coats. These were used to slide down the hill on the ice. There was always a big pile of snow that had fallen from the school house roof, next to the building, so no one had to worry about stopping or running into the building.

The children that did not want to slide on the ice could play in the big covered play shed. Miss Ditto always encouraged everyone to go outside during recess. If there was a student that did not come properly dressed for the cold, Miss Ditto always managed to have extra winter coats and hats in one of the closets. She made sure that every child was dressed properly before allowing them to go outside in cold weather.

It didn't take long for the ruffians to come up with another plan to do something destructive or mischievous at the school. They drove by one morning when we were out sliding on the ice during recess. They evidently could not stand to see us having so much fun so, that night they took axes and grubbing hoes and chopped up the ice and left it in big piles all over the hill side. It froze during the night so we could not clear the ice off. That ended our fun on the ice for several days. Finally, it warmed up and rained and melted the ice. It was only a few days later that the snow came again, and before long we were sliding down the hill by the school again and having fun.

There were days in January and February that it was so cold Miss Ditto would not allow us to go outside, except to go to the outhouse. On those days we played board games, like Chinese checkers, Checkers, and Monopoly. In fact, we were allowed to play Monopoly at other times during the school day. If we finished our lessons in the morning before lunch time, we could go to the back of the room and play Monopoly. I became a Monopoly champion when I got in the 5th grade. I was also pretty good at Checkers. I think my days of playing Monopoly must have had an enduring effect on me, as I have always loved real estate and property, culminating in a 23-year career of selling real estate.

It's a good thing that the State/County allowed 10 snow days each winter. Our little school district used every one of those days during the winters of 1946 through 1948.

CHAPTER XIX

We Get a Visit by A Mountain Lion

By the first of March, the days and nights started getting a little warmer. Rain had pretty much melted most of the snow. My dad decided it was time to butcher the beef steer we had been raising for the last year. As was customary, dad always hung the killed animal up from a tree limb near our front door for a couple of days. He would use a block and tackle, and raise the animal high enough so that cougars or bobcats could not reach the animal and steal the meat. Dad would get up at least once each night to make sure that the killed animal was ok. On the second night dad got up about 1:30 in the morning to check on the animal. When he opened the front door, he saw a mountain lion jumping as high as it could to try to get hold of the leg of the steer. Dad shot into the air with his 22 rifle. He also made a loud whistle, and with that the cougar took off. The steer was untouched. The next morning some of dad's brothers decided they would track the animal. They were able to follow the cougar's tracks for a while, but pretty soon the mountain lion ran through a shallow pond, so the men lost it tracks and returned home. Dad really did not want to kill the mountain lion anyway, he only wanted to scare it away.

The next morning when I went to milk our cow, I was pretty scared. I said, "Dad, would you please go with me to milk the cow?" He said, "No, Son, I've got to leave early this morning, as my shift at the mill starts at 7:30." I then said, "Delbert, will you go with me and hold the lantern?" He said, "Sure, but we will have to hurry as we still need to eat breakfast and get ready for school." In a few days, dad took the steer down, cut it up into steaks, roasts, and made lots of hamburger. We had lots of wonderful, home-grown meat the rest of the winter. Boy, did I have a great story to tell when I got to school Monday morning.

My best friend, Bobby Berge, also had a great story to tell. He and his brothers always carried a rifle with them when they walked to school. They placed the rifle under a log that crossed the little stream they had to cross on their way to school. When they left school on Friday, they picked up their rifle. As they were walking through the woods Bruce spotted a nice four-point buck. He was old enough to have a hunting license and deer tag. He took aim, and with one shot, he had himself a nice kill. This meant that his family would have meat to eat for the rest of the winter.

There were others who had stories to tell, but Miss Ditto rang the bell, and it was time to go inside and begin our studies for the day. Their stories would have to wait 'til morning or noon recess.

I asked some of the Scofield kids if their parents had noticed any gas being taken out of their car's gas tanks. Betty Cartwright said, "Yes, and that's not all, someone stole a brand-new wheelbarrow from my uncle's woodshed the other night. That's really bad because, he does not have the money to buy a new one. He just got laid off from his work planting trees for the Forest Service." I said, "Betty, who is your uncle?" She said "Louie Forest." I went dead silent. I wanted to say it couldn't have happened to a better person, but I didn't because I had a secret crush on Betty. I certainly did not want her to be mad at me.

The Scofield Gang seemed to be pretty quiet for the remainder of March. Things changed in April. Warmer weather seemed to spring them into action.

Upon arriving at school, the second Tuesday in April Bobby Berge told me he had something to tell me at recess. When we got out to the playground he said, "Guess what happened sometime over the weekend?" I said, "What happened, is it bad?" "Yes, it is really bad for my dad." "Why is that?" I said. Bobby responded, "Because someone stole the speeder car that my dad uses to do his job on the railroad, and the company is blaming him, because he did not chain the wheels to the track. He always secures them with a chain but, Friday night he was in a hurry to get home and he failed to make sure the lock was completely closed. When he went to work Monday morning, he discovered the speeder car was gone. This is really bad for our family. Without the speeder car, dad cannot work, and when he doesn't work, we have no money to buy food. The rail road company is going to have the person who has the speeder car in the Buxton section do my dad's section. They told my dad to report the theft to the County Sheriff immediately. So, dad was going to drive to Hillsboro today, and report the theft to the Sheriff's office. I sure hope they do something, but you know they have done very little about the gas stealing that has been going on for some time now." I said, "Yes, I know, and they had better do something about trying to locate your dad's rail road car." With that, we head Miss Ditto ring the bell, so it was time to go back inside and take our seats.

Friday was the last day of school prior to Spring Vacation. Miss Ditto wished everyone to have a good vacation. We were all so excited to get on the bus. When I got on the bus, I noticed that Betty Cartwright was sitting alone in the seat. I asked if she would mind if I sat with her. She smiled and moved over next to the window. I could feel my little heart fluttering in my chest. We talked until the bus arrived at her bus stop. She gave me a cute smile and said, "I'll see you in a week." I was on cloud nine throughout the entire spring vacation.

The highlight of the vacation for the Tophill kids was the arrival of our Uncle Lawrence from the Navy. He was discharged and home for good. We were so happy to see him, and to hear about some of his adventures at sea. He had no civilian clothes as yet, so we got to see him in his dress blues for three or four days. He brought home a folded world map, from which he showed us all of the countries he visited during his time in the Navy. He told us about the time his ship was nearly hit by a torpedo. He told us about visiting Cairo, Egypt and seeing the huge pyramids. He even got to ride on a camel while there.

Uncle Hobert, who was in the Air Force during the war, arrived a few days later. Grandpa and Grandma Long were so happy to have their sons home safe.

The weather was beautiful for most of the vacation. Easter Lilies were in bloom in the forest, and there were edible mushrooms in abundance. Our Mom would not let us bring mushroom into her kitchen, but my Aunt Alice knew which ones were safe to eat, so my cousin, Chan, and I would collect a small grocery sack full and take them to his house. His mother was a wonderful cook. She would clean the mushrooms and then fry then in butter, and we would have a feast.

The days were getting longer, so all of the cousins would spend time in the evenings playing softball or other games. We spent a lot of time in Tarzan's Jungle swinging from tree to tree. My siblings and I would always make at least one trip a day to Grandma Bailey's home. She would always have plenty of good Franz bread, or once in a while she would make homemade bread. We could always go there and have a slice of bread with peanut butter and honey on it. Grandma loved to have us come. Sometimes she would just have us set on her lap, and she would tell us stories about her childhood in South Africa and Holland.

CHAPTER XX

Grandpa Long Opens a Gas Station

The Scofield ruffians never caused any problems in our community of Tophill during the first four days of the vacation but they made up for it on the fifth day. My Grandpa Long had built and opened a small Mobile gas station at the corner of State Highway 47 and Scofield Road, on my Uncle Oscar's property. When his son, Hyrum, arrived early that morning to open for business, he discovered that all of the windows were covered with dried egg yolk. It was very difficult to clean the windows, as we had no electricity or running water in our homes, or at the station at that time. We did not get electricity in our community until 1949 or 1950. Grandpa notified the County Sheriff, Bud Barnes, of the vandalism. He came by that afternoon, but he said there was little he could do, as there was no evidence left at the scene. Grandpa told the sheriff not to worry about it, he was just thankful they did not break any windows. All of us had our suspicions, and we were pretty sure it was the work of the Scofield gang.

In a few hours, Hyrum, Joe and Huey cleaned the egg yolk off the windows, and the station was back in business. We all loved the little station with its big beautiful 'Mobile Gas' flying horse sign. Grandpa sold Franz bread and candy bars. We could buy a loaf of bread for .29 cents and a candy bar for .5 cents. Since there was no electricity, the gasoline had to be pumped into the cars/trucks gas tanks by turning a handle on the pump and filling a reservoir and then it would flow through the hose by gravity into the gas tank.

Life was never dull in our little community. It was so nice to have so many uncles, aunts and cousins close by. Our mothers were all 'stay at home moms'. Most of our dads worked in the large sawmill in Vernonia until the Long boys built their own sawmill. Living so close together also meat there would be disagreements and conflicts among the children from time to time. One time my cousin, Chan, and I got into a scuffle. We both had pocket knives. In the course of the fight, I accidentally cut his hand. This really scared us both. We rushed to his house, and his mom cleaned the wound and put a bandage on it. We never told her how it happened. I felt bad and told my cousin I was sorry. He still has the scar on his hand to this day.

The days flew by, and by Sunday evening we were all excited to be going back to school so we could see our Scofield friends. Miss Ditto greeted each one of us as we got on the bus. I made sure that I sat in a seat all by myself. I was hoping that cute little blond, Betty Cartwright, would set with me, when we got to her bus stop. She never made it down the aisle that far. My sister, Glenda, had also saved a seat for her. As usual, all of us had stories to tell our Scofield friends. Miss Ditto gave us 10 minutes extra for the morning recess.

My best friend, Bobby Berge, handed me a note in class telling me that he had something important to tell me at recess. When we got out side he said, "My father and mother told me last night they were planning on taking the whole family on a trip to Canada next summer." I said, "Really, that would be so exciting." Bobby said, "I can hardly wait, I have not seen my grandparents for five years." Bobby also said, "The trouble makers, you know who I mean don't you? They knocked over several mail boxes in the community this week. I sure wish they would get jobs that would require them to move from our community, or I wish they would all get drafted into the Army." I said, "Bobby, I am with you on everything you said. They were busy in our community also. They put egg yolk on all the windows in my grandpa's service station."

It started raining real hard, so Miss Ditto rang the bell a little early, but when we got inside, she gave us the rest of our recess time to just play board games or just talk. I asked Betty Cartwright if she would like to play me a game of Chinese checkers. She said, "Sure." Unfortunately, we were not able to finish the game, as Miss Ditto said our recess time was up, and that we needed to continue with our school lessons.

It rained a lot during the rest of April, so we either had to play in the play shed or stay in the school building and play board games. The rainy weather seemed to keep the Scofield ruffians in their homes, thank goodness for that. The rain continued on the weekends, so that meant we usually had to stay inside. By the end of April most of the children were really getting 'cabin fever'.

The days were getting longer, and we all knew that meant summer was right around the corner. The old adage, 'April showers bring May flowers' was certainly true this year. The weather turned beautiful in May. We had sunshine almost every day for the first two weeks. The wild flowers were so beautiful, especially the wild Easter lilies. There were also beautiful purple bleeding hearts and many other wild flowers in the forest. The last two weeks of May saw several rainy days. The sunshine and the rain were very good for the strawberry farmers. Al Davies made a trip to Tophill to visit with our parents to make sure the children would be able to help with the berry harvest. The Tophill kids were a big part of his picking crew.

The last day of school finally arrived, so that meant the big party that Miss Ditto had, to celebrate another successful year, would take place on Friday. And yes, the ruffians showed up again. And again, Miss Ditto had to tell them they were not welcome. When they left in their car, they yelled vulgar epitaphs out the car windows.

We were all excited to be out of school for the summer. Everyone passed so, that meant I would be going into fifth grade. We were all hoping that the ruffians would get their jobs back, working for the State Forest, and planting trees in the Tillamook Burn.

I saw my friend, Bobby Berge, a week after school was out at the Buxton store, and he told me that all three of the Scofield Gang members were hired back by the State Forest Service, so that meant we would be free of their mischief for the whole summer, and throughout most of the fall.

CHAPTER XXI

Strawberry Picking Time

Strawberry picking season started early, because of the rain and warm weather. Most of the Tophill kids picked berries for the same farmer, Al Davies, near Banks. Berry picking is hard work, but we all enjoyed doing it. Most of us came from large families, so we were glad to be able to help our parents by making a little extra money during the summer.

Berry picking was also a fun time for most of the children. We got to meet other children from various parts of the country. There were always a few families that were migrant workers. Most of these folks came from Oklahoma, and were referred to as 'Okies.' It didn't matter to us children where they came from, and we became very good friends with many of their children. They were good people and they worked hard. There were many romances that had their beginnings in the berry fields, particularly with the teenagers, both boys and girls. The end of the picking season usually meant the end of the romances.

Summer time also meant a return to many hours of playing with our cousins. Berry season was pretty much over by the 4th of July. Some parents took their children to pick beans, but that was not the case in my family, because my mother did not drive. As usual, the evenings were spent playing games until well after dark. We usually spent at least one afternoon at Tarzan's Jungle, swinging from tree to tree. Another afternoon might be spent building forts in the woods, or just exploring the wild country in which we lived.

Saturday night was always 'bath time'. Mom had a large galvanized round tub. She would heat the water on the stove, as we had no electricity. Each child, starting with the youngest, would strip down, hop into the tub and get a good scrub down. There were seven children in our family at the time. I don't remember Mom ever changing the bath water during 'bath time'.

Sunday was always a special day for most of the Tophill kids. It was 'Church Day.' Moms would get up early and fix breakfast, while the children were getting ready for church. We all attended the same small LDS Branch in Vernonia, which was 10 miles from Tophill. My Dad was the leader of the Branch. After the morning services we returned home. Often, we either had friends from the Branch over to our home for dinner, or we would be invited to their home. Then, we would return to Vernonia for the evening service which usually started about 7:00 p.m. When we got home my father would usually cook a large pot of rice and raisins. We loved Sundays because, we got to see many children who lived in the Vernonia area. Many of the friendships which began in that little Branch lasted for many years. Some even resulted in marriages. We all loved the full-time missionaries that were assigned to our Branch. Most of the time they were sister missionaries.

The summer vacation from school went by so quickly. The end of August meant it was time to go shopping for school clothes. For our family it meant a trip to the huge Montgomery Ward's store in Portland. Dad only took us to one floor, the 2nd story bargain floor. Upon leaving the store there was the annual visit to Dad's Aunt Ada's home in St. Johns. The next Saturday Dad took us to the J.C. Penny store in Forest Grove to buy shoes and other clothes needed to start school. This was an annual event that we always looked forward to.

CHAPTER XXII
Back to School

School always started the day after Labor Day. The first day back was always exciting. Everyone wore their new clothes and shoes. Some kids even got new lunch pails. Miss Ditto always greeted each child as he/she got on the school bus. We were always anxious to see if new children had moved into the school district. I was pleased to see that Betty Cartwright had not moved away. She was just as cute as ever. The wood floors had been re-oiled in the school building. Some of the chalk boards had been replaced. There were two or three new student desks. Some of the walls had a fresh coat of paint. On the playground there were two additional swings and a new teeter totter. Miss Ditto informed us that she had ordered several new softball bats, gloves, and softballs, but they had not arrived yet. The play shed had several new four-square courts with lines painted black. In the coat and lunch pail room there were two new two-gallon milk cans that were used for our drinking water, which had to be hauled from a neighbor each day. There were two new metal drinking cups with long handles. We all used these cups every day.

I was sure happy to see my best friend, Bobby Berge. At recess he told me all about their family vacation to Canada. He was so happy to see his Grand Parents, uncles and aunts, and so many cousins. He also told me about visiting the Banff and Jasper National Parks, and seeing many bears, wolves, Elk and Moose. He also told me that his parents planned to eventually move back to Canada.

Several Scofield parents stopped by to say hi to Miss Ditto and to check out the school building to see what work had been done over the summer. I did hear one parent say that the three trouble makers were still working for the Forest Service planting trees in the Tillamook Burn area.

We were all very happy to have new swings, and new ball equipment on the way. We had five students in the 5th grade this year. There was one new family, the Gamroth family, who had moved into the district.

Western Oregon was enjoying a beautiful late summer and early fall season. Normally it started raining right after Labor Day, but not this year. We were all happy about this kind of weather, because it meant the Forest Service could continue planting trees; thereby keeping the Scofield Ruffians away. This nice fall weather continued clear through the month of September.

When October arrived, we children started thinking about Halloween. Deep snows in the coast range ended the tree planting in the Tillamook burn area, and the Scofield ruffians were back home. One evening, as I was visiting my Uncle Oscar with my father, my uncle said, "Charlie, I wonder what those three hooligans from Scofield will try to pull on us this year on Halloween night?" My father replied, "I don't know, but I don't think they will bother our out houses again, but we better keep an eye on our chicken coops. Since very few of us have garages we had better park our cars very close to our house, and if possible, behind our house." Uncle Oscar agreed and replied, "I am still going to put an electric wire around my outhouse. What about your father-in-law, John Bailey? He is getting pretty old; I hope they don't bother his place." My father replied, "Last year, some of the older teenagers right here in our community did some pretty mean things at John's house. They got his cow out of the barn, put a harness on it, and hooked it up to his hay wagon."

CHAPTER XXIII

The Ruffians Strike at Scofield

The Scofield ruffians wasted no time in planning their next mischievous acts to be carried out on Halloween night. They met together at Staley's Cafe to make a plan. Louie said, "Bill and Harley, I think we had better stay clear of Tophill this Halloween. How about we stay in our own community?" Harley replied, "I think that is a good idea. Let's start at the far end of the community, near the Sunset Highway. I think that is where Mr. Berge lives. I have been wanting to get even with him, ever since he noticed that the switch had been altered on the railroad track that he looks after, last year." Bill said, "We will skip our houses, but hit every other house in the community. That should be loads of fun."

Halloween was on a Thursday, so it was a school night. The parents would be busy with their children until dark. The community was so spread out that it was necessary for parents to drive their children trick or treating. There was a little snow on the ground, and it was very cold. The ruffians met at Bill's place. They decided they would make a drive through the community to make sure all the children were through trick or treating, and in their homes. They had no trouble finding the Berge's outhouse, and fortunately their dogs were not outside. The outhouse was a way from the road, but they made it back to their car without being noticed. The next house belonged to Mr. Bedford Loftis. The ruffians parked their car on the opposite side of the road. Again, they had no trouble finding the outhouse. The next house belonged to Mr. and Mrs. Atwood. Just as they got out of their car and started to approach the front gate, two big German Shepherd dogs came running at full speed. Louie slammed the gate close just in time, and they made a beeline for their car. Louie and Bill made it to the car but Harley was not so lucky. The lead dog went through a hole in the fence, caught up with Harley and grabbed his pant leg, and down he went. Bill grabbed a steel bar, which was lying on the floor board in the back seat of their car, and ran to assist his fallen comrade. He hit the dog, and with that the dog let go of his pant leg, and Harley was able to get back to the car. His leg was bleeding, and upon closer examination the dog had taken a chunk of flesh from his lower leg. That ended their mischievous deeds for this Halloween night. Harley's comment was, "Now we have another family to get even with." Bill said, "Harley, you can't blame the Atwood's, most of the families in our neighborhood have dogs, and they were just trying to protect their owner's property." Harley said, "Bill you are right. Just get me home so I can get this wound cleaned up and a bandage put over it. I sure hope I don't get an infection."

The Tophill kids had a great time going to one another's homes and collecting loads of candy. The weather was decent, meaning it was not raining or snowing. No one bothered Grandpa Bailey's place that year. There were still a few outhouses tipped over, but that was the work of the older teen age, Long family boys.

The weather turned quite cold in November. As usual, my dad had been so busy with working at the sawmill, that he had not been able to get our winter supply of wood in. Thankfully, Grandpa Bailey always came to our rescue. He had wood delivered from the mill in Vernonia, so if we got desperate, we could always get wood from grandpa. There were times when we would go out to the nearby woods and peel off large chunks of bark from old stumps to burn in our wood heating stove. I can also remember times when me and Delbert, and sometimes my older sisters, would go with Dad to the mill slab pile, start up the buzz saw, and cut enough wood to last a week or two. I can never remember going into the winter months with a supply of dry wood, nor did we have a wood shed to keep wood in.

We were all excited to have a few days off from school for Thanksgiving. It had been snowing off and on for several days. By Thanksgiving Day, we had about 12 inches of snow on the ground. Our family always had a big Thanksgiving Dinner and we would invite Grandma and Grandpa Bailey for dinner. Grandpa Bailey built us some sleds out of 2 by 4's, which he brought to us when they came for dinner. The other Top Hill families always had great Thanksgiving dinners. My father, being the leader of our little branch of the LDS Church, always made sure that families in our branch that were out of work or low on funds, had food to prepare a Thanksgiving dinner. He was able to draw from funds that members contribute for helping the poor. Another organization within the church, known as the Relief Society, was also able to assist with providing assistance to families that were having difficult times with illness or other unforeseen problems.

CHAPTER XXIV

The Gang Continue Their Pranks at Tophill

The Scofield ruffians decided that things were entirely too quiet and peaceful. Louie drove his car over to Bill's house, and together they drove to Harley's house. Louie said, "Guys, I have been thinking about having some fun with those Top Hill folks. Since we have had a lot of snow, why don't we put the snow blade on my jeep, and go plow their drive ways full of snow? We could go tonight about midnight." Bill and Harley thought this was a great idea. It took about an hour to put the snow blade on Louie's four-wheel drive jeep. Bill told Harley and Louie that he would buy their dinner if they would like to go down to Staley's cafe in Buxton. At 11:30 p.m. they drove to Tophill and spent the next two hours completing their dirty little deeds of mischief. Not one single car passed during the entire time of their mischief. They piled at least 2 feet of snow in every drive way. They got the snow from the side of the road. State Highway snow plows had been keeping the roads clear for several days, so there were high banks of snow along the road sides.

When my father got up to go work, he got a big surprise when he tried to leave our driveway. He had to go back to the house and get a shovel and clear the snow away. It is a good thing he always left early, as it took him about 20 minutes to remove the snow. When he went to pick us his brothers and one brother-in-law, he found that all of their driveways were also filled with snow. They did not have time to clear everyone's driveway, or they would have been late to get to their jobs at the Oregon American Sawmill in Vernonia. To my knowledge, they never did find out who did this dirty little mischievous deed.

The next morning, Louie picked up Bill and Harley, and drove to Vernonia via Tophill. They were very pleased to see that all the driveways except one was still piled full of snow. It continued to snow off and on for the first two weeks of December, but not enough to close the schools. The Tophill kids were beginning to get excited about Christmas and being out of school for a couple of weeks, and I am sure the Scofield kids shared the same excitement. We had spent almost every afternoon at school preparing for the Christmas program. Miss Ditto loved to be able to present this program to both communities every year. My hope was that neither of the Scofield gang members would show up the night of the program.

CHAPTER XXV

A Wonderful Christmas for Little Mary

December the 21st finally arrived, the last day of school for two weeks. We did one last full-dress rehearsal. Miss Ditto asked one last time if every child was going to be able be at the school for their part in the program. One little first grade girl raised her hand and said, "Miss Ditto, I don't think I will be able to come, you see my Mommy is very sick, and my Daddy got laid off at the sawmill last week." With that my older sister raised her hand and said, "I am sure my parents would be happy to stop by your house and bring you with us. If they would let you, you could even spend the night at our house." Little Mary started to cry. Miss Ditto called her up to her desk, put her arms around her, and said, "Mary, don't you worry, things will all work out." And they did work out. As soon as me and my siblings got home from school, my sister asked my dad if we could stop by Mary's house and bring her with us to the Christmas program. My dad readily agreed that we could pick Mary up, and he also said if her here parents would let her, she could stay overnight at our house.

The Christmas program went off without a hitch. Santa Claus made his usual appearance at the end of the program. He gave each child a stocking filled with popcorn balls, an orange and some chocolate kisses. With a *Ho! Ho! Ho!* and a Merry Christmas to all, he exited out the back door of the school building.

CHAPTER XXVI

The Gang Finally Become Good Citizens

All three members of the Scofield Gang came to the program with their parents, and believe it or not, they behaved themselves and seemed to really enjoy the program.

We had snow almost every day of the vacation. On the last Friday of the vacation, a warming trend came to our area. The famous Chinook Winds came earlier this year. By Sunday night, most of the snow had melted, in fact there was some flooding in the town of Vernonia, and we were not able to go to church. To my knowledge, the Scofield Gang caused no problems during the entire vacation. Who knows, maybe there are starting to grow up and act like mature adults.

We were all very happy to be back in school. As usual, Miss Ditto gave us some extra time at the first recess, so we could hear about all the things our friends did during the holiday.

The rest of the school years went by very fast. Sure enough, the ruffians caused no trouble in either community during the rest of the school year. In June, all three of the ruffians got hired as full-time employees of the State Forest Service. This meant they were able to settle down and become responsible citizens at last, and thus ends our story of 'The Scofield Gang.'

ABOUT THE AUTHOR

I was born in 1938 in Brigham City, Utah. My parents moved to Oregon in the early spring of 1941, prior to the United States entering World War II.

I grew up in the foot hills of the Coast Range Mountains of Western Oregon near the small town of Buxton. I was the oldest son of a family of nine children, five boys and four girls. My father and his brothers operated a small sawmill and logging company for many years and my mother worked very hard as a stay-at-home mom.

I attended a small rural elementary school located in the tiny community of Scofield, Oregon. We had one teacher for all eight grades. The average yearly enrollment was about 20 to 29 students. We had no electricity in the school building or in the neighboring community of Tophill, where I lived. We had an outhouse for the boys on one end of the property and one for the girls on the other end. The school building was heated with a large wood burning stove in one corner of the room. The lights were kerosene lamps which, I believe, hung from the ceiling.

I was very young during those war years, but I do remember several things about those years. I remember the times we had to put newspaper over our windows at night to keep the light from shining through to the outside, just in case there were enemy planes flying overhead. I also remember the rationing stamps my parents used to be able to buy many things for our family like sugar, gasoline, and many other products.

I also remember my favorite Uncle Lawrence joining the Navy to help in the war effort. Oh, how we all loved our uncle and most of us cried when he left, not knowing if we would ever see him alive again. I remember the first time he came home on leave. He was wearing his beautiful Navy Blue Uniform of which he was so proud. I decided right then and there that I wanted one of those uniforms. Shortly after that my parents went to the local J.C. Penny store in Forest Grove and bought me a little boys Navy outfit. I was so proud. I decided, at a very early age, that when I grew up I wanted to be a Sailor just like my Uncle Lawrence.

Fast forward to January of 1957. I realized my dream and joined the Navy at the young age of 18 years old. I did my boot camp at the Naval Training Center in San Diego, California. My first duty assignment was at the Naval Air Station in Jacksonville, Florida. From there I was transferred on board the USS New DDE 818 whose home port was Norfolk, Va.

Fast forward again to about the year 2000. My grandchildren wanted me to tell them stories of things that I experienced while I was in Uncle Sam's Navy. From that point on they were known as Grandpa's Old Navy Stories. These were always bed time stories and I would usually fall asleep before finishing the story. The children would shake my arm and say "Grandpa, wake up! We want to hear the rest of the story." Most of the time I would tell them that I was just too sleepy but that I would finish the story the next time they came to our home for a sleep-over. Amazingly, they could always remember exactly where I left on. You can rest assured, I could never remember, as I had to create the story as I told it. Every story had a title which represented a different experience, some longer than others. Unfortunately, but also fortunately, the grandchildren are all older now so I have no one to tell these stories to until the great grandchildren come into our lives.

EPILOGUE

Both communities, Scofield and Tophill, Orgon are still small with the same gravel road leading from Tophill to Scofield. The school operated until about 1958. A new school was built about one half mile closer to Tophill, but it only operated a couple years. People in the community voted to consolidate with a larger neighboring district, Buxton, Oregon. One room Schools are pretty much a thing of the past. Anyone that went to Scofield during those years is now probably 70 years old or older. The author of this book is now 85 years old and lives in Texas. He still has 5 of his siblings alive and doing well.

ABOUT THE AUTHOR

Mel came from a family of nine children, he being the oldest son. Mel attended this little one room school through grade seven. Over half of the students in Scofield School were either brothers and sisters or first cousins. His teacher for all those years was Erie E. Ditto. Many of the events in this book actually happened. Other events are the imagination of the author. This is the second book Mel has authored. His first book was titled "The Mistry Of Goat Mountain and still available on Amazon.

www.ingramcontent.com/pod-product-compliance
Lightning Source LLC
LaVergne TN
LVHW091600060526

83820OLV00036B/931